Planting Design

Theodore D. Walker

PDA Publishers Corporation
Mesa, Arizona

Copyright © 1985 by Theodore D. Walker

Library of Congress Cataloging in Publication Data

Walker, Theodore D.
    Planting design.

    Includes index.
    1. Landscape gardening.   2. Landscape architecture.
I. Title.
SB472.W24   1985   712'.6   84-26522
ISBN 0-914886-30-4

P D A PUBLISHERS CORPORATION
1725 East Fountain
Mesa, Arizona 85203

Contents

1

Introduction

Plants have been a part of our earth for a very long time and are a source of oxygen, food, fuel and building materials for the benefit of man. Besides these functional uses they also add much to the aesthetic appearance of our natural environment. Man seems to have an inherent affinity for plants and has brought them into his everyday living and working environment.

In the decades since World War II we have witnessed increased interest in quality landscape development, and this has provided many opportunities for planting designers. This interest ranges from the small scale of the homeowner up to the large scale of strip mine restoration. More plants are being used around home, offices, factories, and parking lots. There is a greater sensitivity to preserving existing vegetation and harmonizing new design efforts with it.

Plant breeders are working continually to create dwarf and improved selections of familiar plants to be used in smaller spaces and adverse situations. They also breed and select for larger flowers, fruits, and disease resistance. These improvements provide the designer with a better selection of plants for use in planting design. In recent years there has been an emphasis on the use of indigenous plants to harmonize with the natural environment. Many have good potential for design use, and nurseries are beginning to propagate and stock them to enable the designer to specify them.

Planting design involves function as well as beauty. The designer will need to be familiar with all aspects of the site such as location in relation to climatic influences, location of structures (heat, reflection, shade patterns, etc.), underground and overhead utilities (affects the location of trees, etc.), circulation patterns of people and vehicles, drainage patterns including groundwater tables, and the unique needs of the client, and others.

Once you have become familiar with design principles you will realize that much of our man-made landscape is poorly designed and maintained. Too much planting is done by those who have had no training in design principles. Plants are placed where they interfere with attractive views, where they block essential line of sight at street intersections, or they break up usable space. Plants are used which grow too large for the space they occupy and they crowd sidewalks or block the light into windows. Maintenance costs are increased when the wrong plants are selected or placed in the wrong locations. Many plant grouping fail to harmonize with the lines, forms, and spaces created by structures (the architectural design), and the walls, paving, fountains, other site features, and topography of the site.

As an art form planting design differs from others in that it is always changing. Plants continually grow. Unlike the sculptor whose work is finished after the last of the stone is chipped away, the initial planting design will not have the form envisioned by the designer. It will emerge as the plants grow, and the final effects may be affected by disease, unusual weather or poor maintenance or neglect, most of which are outside the control of the designer.

If the user of this book does not have a basic understanding of plant growth, plant ecology and plant nomenclature, it would be well to pursue an elementary introduction to botany and horticulture before proceeding. It is essential to understand how light, temperature, water, soils, and nutrients affect the life and growth of plants.

The purpose of this book is to furnish the user with some basic principles to improve the use of plants in man's environment. First we will study the principles of design as they apply to the use of plants. The functional uses and aesthetic values of plants will be explained in the next two chapters. In the fourth chapter the process of planting design is explored and, it is followed by two chapters which cover the preparation of planting plans and specifications. This book has been profusely illustrated as it is easier to comprehend and understand design if one can see it as well as read about it.

2

Design Principles

When using plants in the landscape, anyone who designs a landscape applies some basic principles of design, which are common also to other design professions, including architecture, interior design, and other arts. These principles consist in various uses of line, form, texture, color, repetition, variety, balance, and emphasis; all of these terms apply to any aesthetic composition or work of art. In planting design some specific functions must also be considered along with aesthetic development. These functional factors will be discussed in Chapter 3.

The design of the landscape has unique qualities that distinguish it from other works of art, however. Whereas a painting is created on the flat surface of a canvas and a piece of sculpture is intended to be viewed on a pedestal, the designed landscape can be walked through, around, and under. In most arts, the beholder has to focus his senses toward an aesthetic effect that has been produced in a condensed or restricted space, but in landscape design the beholder can experience the artistic effect in many diverse ways, because he is within the design. Its scale is his scale. In a properly designed landscape, scale can be measured in relation to the size of people and the sizes of the spaces they need for their activities.

Furthermore, the landscape composition changes as one moves through it and is constantly modified by ever-changing shadows as the sun crosses the sky, by the movements of clouds, by the emergence and disappearance of vistas relative to the viewer, and by the changing nature of the plants: new leaves in the spring, the appearance and aroma of flowers and fruit, the transformations of color in the fall, and the bareness of branches in winter.

Adding complexity to the three-dimensional composition of the landscape is a multitude of other factors from the physical environment, discussed elsewhere in this book. In his efforts, the designer faces tremendous challenge to create a work of art that is aesthetically pleasing to all the senses, is functional, and is harmonious with the physical environment in which it must survive, too.

AESTHETIC BASES OF LANDSCAPE DESIGN

Line. When the designer wants to create or control patterns, he does so by making use of line. The lines he has envisioned may ultimately become edges and borders. In a landscape composition a carefully planned group of lines will direct the attention of the viewer to a focal point or a particular area of interest in the composition. Lines are also useful in controlling movement, either visual or physical, in straight or curved directions. Rows of plants such as hedges are one example of the use of lines, but a row of trees may also create a line that is different because of the size and character of the trees. Moreover, lines can be found in the edges of paving materials as well as in the patterns in the material itself. Other kinds of lines are emphasized with fences and walls.

In nature there is a line, but it is less well defined or not as strong as lines created by the edge of pavement or a wall. It may be just the point of separation of leaf color or texture which creates an imaginary line by the eye.

Whereas the line created by the edge of paving can be relatively simple, complex lines can occur in nature such as deciduous trees in winter where lines move in several directions at once. There are horizontal lines, vertical lines, lines moving toward the viewer, lines moving away from the viewer, to the left, to the right, etc. In other words, three-dimensional. Some lines run parallel while others intersect.

Straight lines suggest direct movement without hesitation. Interconnecting straight lines create points at the intersections for hesitation, stopping, sitting, changes of views, and reflections back to the point of beginning. Meandering, curved lines invite slower movement and are useful in areas that should seem natural as possible, such as a path through the woods.

2.1 Four rows of trees, create straight lines which run parallel to the sides and perpendicular to the ends of this garden area at the Fort Worth Museum of Art.

2.2 Lines intersecting at an angle in this paved area on the campus of the University of California, Los Angeles.

2.2

2.3 Curvilinear lines expressed in the paving, lights and bulletin board at Bitzer Park in North Canton, Ohio.

2.4 Meandering lines appear in nature at the point of abrupt transition between evergreen and deciduous growth. Caribou National Forest, Idaho.

2.4

2.5 *Meandering lines intentionally created to simulate nature in a dry-style residential landscape at Tucson, Arizona.*

2.6 *The individual vertical forms of a plant may be merged when they are planted close together to create a horizontal form such as a hedge.*

2.7 *An example of the massing of plants to create horizontal forms. This view is enframed by the vertical forms of the adjacent trees. Samuel Park, Dallas, Texas.*

Form. The result of the total mass of a plant or its outline against the sky is described with the term "form." The trunk, branches, and leaves together create a form. It has mass because it occupies space. Deciduous plants have more visual mass and their form is more strongly defined when in leaf. When the leaves have fallen, the mass is weaker and the form is less defined.

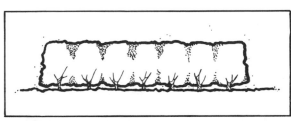

2.6

The importance of form in design is dependent upon being able to see it. In a small scale situation such as a residence, the form of a large tree is relatively unimportant when you are under it and using it for shade.

If a plant is tall and slender, it is said to have vertical form. If it is low and spreading, it is said to have a horizontal form. A group of vertical plants may be grouped together in sufficient quantity so that the length of the group is greater than the height and thus creating a horizontal form (that is after the plants have grown sufficiently that there is no space between them and their individual forms have disappeared). A hedge of upright yews is just one example.

2.7

6

2.8 A sunken garden area adjacent to a shopping center in Atlanta, Georgia. Horizontal forms created from the massing of plants repeat the angular lines of the design.

2.9 Through careful training plants can be espaliered against a vertical surface such as a wall or fence.

Some shrubs with dense foliage can be trimmed into sculptured forms called "topiary" a practice rather uncommon today because of high labor costs but quite popular in seventeenth-century Dutch and English gardens. Rather than topiary many homeowners today just trim their shrubs into boxes, mounds or globes whereas most landscape architects prefer natural plant forms. These may be identified and described as columnar, upright, pyramidal, round, vase-shaped, vertical-oval, horizontal-oval and flat-spreading. These are illustrated in Chapter 5.

2.9

2.10

2.11

2.12

Texture. A designer tries to emphasize various textures through his use of plants and other landscape materials. It is common to express the texture of plants in gradations from fine to medium to coarse. In an area that is to be planted with ground-covering plants, the large leaves of heartleaf bergenia (*Bergenia cordifolia*) present a coarse texture in contrast to Japanese pachysandra (*Pachysandra terminalis*), a plant with medium texture, and Irish moss or moss sandwort (*Arenaria verna* var. *caespitosa*), which has a fine texture. For contrast, pea gravel will provide a fine texture against the coarse texture of a group of large boulders averaging two or more feet in diameter.

Deciduous plants may yield a different texture when their leaves are off. Whereas they may exhibit a fine texture in summer, their winter branching may give an impression of coarseness.

While texture in design is largely a visual characteristic it may also be felt by the skin of the fingers when in close contact with a plant. Some leaves will feel smooth while others will be rough. Bark also ranges from very smooth to very coarse to the touch.

2.10 Low growing plants used as ground cover create low horizontal forms. The rigid lines of the sidewalk have been softened by the plant material overgrowing the edge.

2.11, 2.12 Some plants will naturally grow up a wall without any training needed, but the form will be irregular rather than formal as with a trained espalier.

2.13

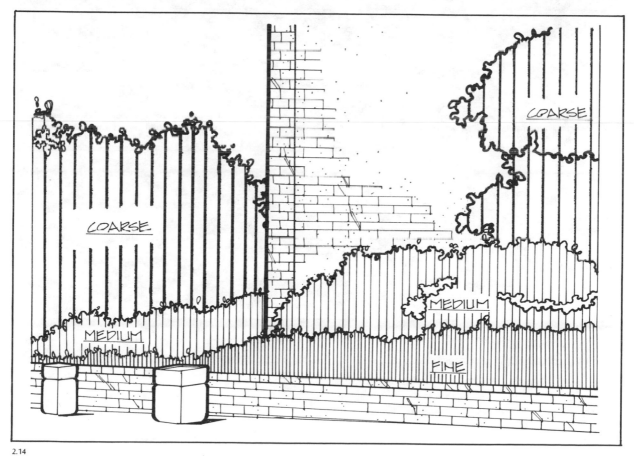

2.14

2.13 The plant in the foreground is fine-textured with a medium-textured shrub behind it and the trees are a little coarser.

2.14 Graphic technique for analyzing and illustrating the texture in Figure 2.13.

2.15 *The ivy ground cover could be considered fine-textured in the particular instance or it might be classified as a medium-texture against the coarse texture of the remaining plants.*

2.16 *A strong contrast between two textures.*

2.17 *The textures of the juniper and pine naturally complement the coarseness of the rock.*

2.16

2.17

2.18 *Changes in foliage color can add interest and contrast to the landscape.*

Color. Most people, in one way or another, find that color has emotional impact. But human response to individual colors varies, and behavioral scientists find it difficult to measure and evaluate that response. In general, reds, oranges, and yellows are considered warm colors and seem to advance toward the viewer. Greens and blues are cooler colors and tend to recede in a composition. Dark blue, a cool color, may thus become a background color in compositions made up of several colors. Gray, being neutral, is best of all as a background when bright colors are used in the foreground. Numerous books have been written on color theory and a would-be designer does well to look into some of them if he does not know much about the nature of color.

In the landscape nearly everything expresses color, and colors seldom seem constant. There is almost an infinite variety of greens in leaves. Even in one species the green of the leaves undergoes a considerable change from the light, fresh color of an emerging new leaf in spring to the darker tones of midsummer and change completely from green to another color when fall arrives. Flowers and fruit also provide a wide variety of color. Winter colors tend to be more stark; bark colors and their variation will be more noticeable and will be accented by the color of persistent fruit, along with the greens of evergreen plants. Color is affected by light. Flowers in the afternoon shade reflect color differently than when the morning sun is shining on them. Shade subdues the intensity of the color. Darker colors, especially dark blues becomes very subdued in shade. In complete shade where the light levels are very low all day, most plants will not flower making flower color considerations irrelevant.

11

2.19

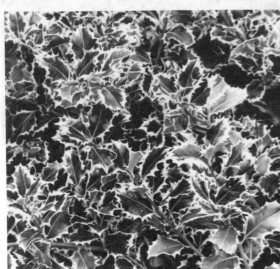

2.20

2.21

2.22

2.23

2.19 – 2.24 Additional examples of foliage color.

Leaf color, however, is another matter, except that those that change in the autumn from green to orange or yellow or red will not be as brilliant or change color at all in shade. Sun reflecting from leaves enhances their surface color. While standing under a tree with the sun overhead, leaves appear translucent and leaf color is lighter and brigher, evoking a strong emotional resonse of beauty.

Nature's colors are nearly always superior to those manufactured by man and are subtler. Designers must be sensitive to color and know how to utilize it as one of the variables in designing the landscape.

12

2.24

Variety. A critical element in design is variety: too little leads to monotony and too much brings confusion. A very fine balance between extremes produces a pleasant sense of unity in a landscape composition. A planting design containing only junipers, even though these have a variety of forms and sizes, can be monotonous because the texture of junipers is so uniform. So far, in all terms we have discussed, we have stressed that a variety of lines, forms, textures, and colors is needed to create an orderly, interesting landscape. But this does not mean that every shrub and every tree must be different within a design.

2.25 Both variety and a repetition were successfully used with the plant materials in this sitting area on the campus of the University of California at Los Angeles.

2.25

13

2.26

2.28

2.27

2.29 *Repetition of similar plant forms to create horizontal masses which lend to unity and harmony in the landscape. This is at Samuel Park in Dallas, Texas.*

2.26 A relatively small scale garden area at Sea World in San Diego where considerable variety was used with little repetition.

2.27 A low planting of spreading yews and the vertical form of a straight row of honey locust repeat the lines created by the paving and light fixtures at Fort Wayne, Indiana City Hall.

2.28 A row of shrubs and a row of trees repeat the circular line of the fountain on the left.

Repetition. Repetition gives the element of variety meaning and expression. It reduces the confusion that may result from excessive variety and introduces a sense of order to the viewer of the landscape. Designers frequently use the word "order" to describe a pleasing design.

Repetition is usually achieved by placing individual plants in groups or masses of a single species. In a large-scale landscape these masses, of varying sizes, may be repeated as the designer finds necessary.

14

Balance. Usually it is possible to perceive a central axis in a landscape composition. When weight, numbers, masses, etc., are distributed equally on both sides of the central axis, the composition is said to be in balance. It is on the basis of balance that landscapes are judged to be formal and informal, or symmetrical and asymmetrical. In a formal landscape, the distribution on either side of the axis is likely to be exactly the same, plant by plant. Except in a few public gardens, there are few formal landscape designs in existence today. Since World War II informality has been more popular. In informal landscapes the balance is likely to be equivalent rather than exact, and a large plant on one side of the axis may balance with a number of smaller plants on the other.

2.30

2.30 The repetition and close spacing of these trees create a sense of enclosure as though you were in a room.

2.31 Asymmetrical balance between the plant materials and the horizontal and vertical forms of the planters and paving are achieved with this design.

2.31

2.32 An example of formal or symmetrical balance, in the recreated garden of William Bryan, Colonial Williamsburg, Virginia.

2.33 Another example of asymmetrical balance in the entrance planting to Bernheim Forest in Kentucky.

2.34 A cluster of birches was placed as the focal point in this east coast residential garden.

2.32   Colonial Williamsburg Foundation

2.34   A. E. Bye and Associates

2.35

2.37

2.36

2.35 *The light-colored foliage of this plant stands as a point of emphasis at the National Arboretum in Washington, D.C.*

2.36 *The strong form and striking individual character of this plant serves as a focal point or point of emphasis in the landscape.*

2.37 *At the Sonora Desert Museum near Tucson, Arizona, this organ cactus (Lemaireocereus thurberi) acts as a point of emphasis.*

Emphasis. Through the use of emphasis, the eye is directed to one portion or object of the composition. This could be a single tree, a group of shrubs with unique character, or some structural feature, perhaps a fountain or a piece of sculpture. Secondary points of emphasis may be used too, whereby the eye is directed toward plants or other landscape features that have less contrast with the overall composition than the primary point or area of emphasis has.

MAN'S PERCEPTION OF THE LANDSCAPE

To perceive one's environment is to become aware of it through the senses of seeing, hearing, touching, smelling, and tasting (though taste is relatively unimportant in the perception of the landscape). Perception is also the process of communication by which an individual learns about himself and others and about other life and objects on the planet Earth. In the preceding paragraphs we spoke frequently of visual aspects of the landscape. Considering that other senses beside vision are important in perceiving the landscape, the "viewer" is actually a "participant" in the landscape.

2.38 The sun is reflected brightly from the snow and provides strong contrast to the dark foliage of the conifers. Silence is broken by the snow-fed brook. A winter scene at Lake Tahoe, California.

2.39 Stand of old growth redwood, Del Norte County, California. A forest such as this creates an imcomparable feeling of serenity. The size of these trees is revealed by the human in the lower left of the photo.

Interaction of the Senses. Very little perception of the landscape occurs without some interaction of all the senses. As a means of examining this idea, think about the extent to which the following descriptions are made up of knowledge gained from sensory perception. All "landscape" is divided into natural and man-made categories. In scale, the natural landscape ranges from mountains and oceans to trees and ponds and to sticks, stones, and alpine flowers. The man-made lanscape ranges in scale from city parks to village squares, from university campuses to shopping-center malls, from neighborhood miniparks to residential gardens.

What is perceived is dependent upon time, place, and particular sets of circumstances. Any landscape will contain some structural elements. Structural elements such as rocks and well-built buildings in the landscape change slowly through time. Plant life becomes established and semipermanent through time, changing seasonally, and emerging, living, and dying as part of the cycle of life. The atmosphere above any landscape changes constantly as the air shifts from place to place. Temperatures fluctuate and clouds soften the sun's shadows and lessen its heat.

All the senses interact during a walk in the autumn, after the leaves have started to fall. The eyes detect the movement of the leaves, both those that are falling and those being shuffled by the feet. At the same time, reinforcing the visually perceived data, the sense of touch is stimulated as leaves are stepped on and brush against the ankles and shoes. A light autumn drizzle begins: the freshly fallen leaves emit a dry, earthy odor.

Now imagine wintertime. It is a cold, crisp morning. A few inches of snow have fallen and the sun is shining. The visual sense is affected by the brightness of the sun's rays reflected from the snow. A slight breeze bites the cheeks and dries the nostrils. Some effort is required to move the feet through the snow. The sensation is reinforced by the crunching sound of the snow, detected by the ears. One's equilibrium is tested by occasional slick spots of ice.

Adaptation of the Senses. After prolonged exposure to certain sensations, such as odors, the body makes an adaptation; the mind responds less to a stimulus and it may even go unnoticed. A bouquet of flowers placed on the table in the dining room produces a pleasant odor throughout the room that will not be noticeable after a few hours because adaptation has occurred. If one leaves the room for a few hours or takes a breath of fresh air outdoors and then returns to the room, the odor will be perceived again as if new. During its evolution, the human nervous system developed the ability to adapt to continuous, repetitive stimuli in order to keep the senses sharp for important new sensory information.

The sensory stimuli provided by the landscape are so varied that there is less monotony of perception or need for adaptation than in any other of man's physical environments. There are daily changes of the landscape in summer as flowers emerge and die to be replaced by fruit. Seasonal changes cover bare branches with leaves; the leaves, in turn, change from light green in spring to the brilliant colors of autumn. Whereas buildings remain static, the landscape is forever changing as plants grow and gain in size, modifying the scale of their surrounding spatial environment.

Modifications of Perception. As the landscape is perceived, the brain interprets the input. That interpretation is modified by previous experience. Once your finger has been painfully pricked by a rose thorn, your memory recall system, which is active during perception, is likely to caution you against blundering into other rose thorns.

Memory recall will also help one to enjoy pleasant experiences. Once one has had the extremely pleasant experience of walking through a natural landscape, such as a group of virgin woods in early spring when the wildflowers are in full bloom and the tree leaves are beginning to emerge, memory recall will influence you to repeat the experience when the same conditions recur the next year.

However, psychological theorizing has yet to explain the pleasurable feeling that comes when one walks through the serenity of some woods on a warm, fresh spring morning. It is just as difficult to explain the pleasure of the sounds of a Bach toccata reverberating in an ancient cathedral.

Night Effects. When night arrives, the amount of information the eyes receive is reduced even though the iris of the eye opens up to let in more light. The distance the eye can see at night varies according to the amount of artificial lighting available and the amount of natural lighting from the moon. Considerable distances can be seen during a full moon on an open snow-covered countryside.

Perception is altered by strong and long shadows. Further alteration comes during and after a rain, when wet surfaces reflect light in many directions.

Attention. A single person walking through the landscape will be affected more by his environment and will perceive more detail in it than will two or more persons who are involved with conversation while they walk. If one person is wandering slowly or meandering, several details are apt to catch his attention. If he has a goal in mind during his walk and is hurrying towards it, several things in the landscape will probably escape his attention.

TOTAL DESIGN DEVELOPMENT

So far we have described some design principles and some aspects of man's perception of the landscape. Now it will be helpful to know how a skillful designer tries to combine all of these things into a total design development.

Composing a work of art requires training and practice. An accomplished pianist only achieved such success through rigorous training and extended practice at the keyboard. So too, a good landscape designer becomes such through thorough training and practicing his art form. Time is required as one does not acquire these skills overnight.

While design is a process that includes analyzing and accommodating the needs of a client and working within the constraints or existing conditions of the site, there is still plenty of room for the intuitive portion of the design process and the opportunity for creating a work of art.

All of the design principles are combined to one degree or another in a planting design but the designer simultaneously gives consideration to the functional problems and needs of the landscape project. Then, aesthetic solutions to landscape problems are developed through a process that is more or less intuitive, depending upon the background, training, and experience of the designer. A designer with considerable experience may find that a design that is aesthetically successful comes largely by intuition.

Most planting designs are influenced by facilities either existing at the site or being designed as part of the project. The use the designer makes of line, form, texture, color, repetition, and emphasis must be closely coordinated with the use the architect has made of the same elements in the architecture at the site and with any land surfaces, walls, fences,

2.40 The angles of the building are repeated in the angles in the paving. There is careful placement and repetition of plant masses to create overall design harmony. This is on the campus of Arizona State University at Tempe, Arizona.

2.41, 2.42 Two views of a private residential garden on Long Island, a contrast of shadows, texture and forms changes as one moves from one part of the garden to another. Subtle, undulating lines soften the flatness of the foreground (man-made ground forms) and clumps of bayberry provide additional interest in the composition. The view across the garden is terminated by a mixture of deciduous and evergreen trees. Winter provides additional patterns and contrasts.

2.41

2.42

2.43

2.44

2.43 – 2.46 *Several views of a Connecticut residential garden designed to stay in scale over many years, to possess a quality of space that is intimate, colorful, and welcoming, and to require little maintenance. Contrast is achieved between the hardness of the rocks and the softness of the plants, yet there is unity or harmony between the horizontal and mounded forms of each. Plant materials, include Japanese red pine (Pinus densiflora), eastern white pine (P. strobus), Japanese black pine (P. thunbergii), shore juniper (Juniperus conferta), andorra juniper (J. chinensis 'sargentii'). Spreading English yew (Taxus baccata 'repandens') is used for accent and emphasis.*

2.45   A. E. Bye and Associates

2.46   A. E. Bye and Associates

paving materials and patterns, planters, pools, benches, etc. All must become part of the total landscape design of the site; as an integral part of the design, they provide three-dimensional relief to a landscape and cannot be separated during aesthetic and functional considerations of the use of plants.

Use of plant and landscape materials as design elements must also be coordinated with their use to fulfill functional needs of the project, which may or may not include the need for visual and physical barriers, climate control (of shade or of wind, etc.), noise control, erosion control, etc. How plants fulfill these functions is discussed in Chapter 3.

The functional aspects of a landscape design may dictate the location and size of plant masses on a site and may, indeed, affect the total aesthetic composition. Whatever their effect, the designer judges each part of the total design in terms of line, form, texture, color, repetition, and emphasis so that these design elements will still be successfully implemented to create a pleasing aesthetic effect on all of man's perceptual senses.

Plant Masses. The designer should try to achieve a transition in his design in order to relate large vertical plant masses to horizontal plants. A pyramidal effect can be created by using smaller plants in front of larger ones so that the plant mass will descend in size from the largest plant to the smallest. This technique also provides the advantage of covering up unsightly bare spots at the bases of large shrubs. The descending pyramidal effect is also used in isolated large masses in order to make a gradual transition from a high point in the center of the mass to a low level on the edges of the mass. Large plant masses usually have the pleasantest effect if viewed from a distance. Designing large plant masses close to both sides of a pedestrian corridor produces an uncomfortable feeling for most people.

A designer should try to provide transitions in texture. Abrupt changes from fine to coarse texture within a single plant mass will not be as aesthetically pleasing as a gradual transition, because the difference in texture will emphasize the individuality of plants rather than the unity of the plant mass. How often such transitions should occur depends upon the scale of the project and the effects being sought by the designer. In a small-scale project, one plant with very coarse texture might be utilized as a focal point in the composition. Gradual textural transitions would then be wanted between

2.47

2.48

2.47 Large masses of plantings are in scale with large spaces such as Samuel Park, in Dallas, Texas. The grass area to the right is screened from the adjacent road and parking to the left.

2.48 The planting harmonizes with the form and character of the architecture to form a unified work of art at the Health Cener of San Diego State University.

24

2.49

2.50

2.49 *Repetition and balance have been achieved in this planting composition at Scottsdale, Arizona.*

2.50 *In a small scale planting more variety and less repetition is desirable in order to achieve the desired results.*

other plant masses in the composition so as not to attract the eye away from the point of emphasis in the composition. In a large-scale project, the point of emphasis may be a large mass of plants or a grouping of objects. Gradual textural transition throughout all subordinated plant masses may then be more important than a transition within each individual mass of plants.

Seasonal stability and variety is accomplished in plant masses through a mix of deciduous and evergreen plants (either coniferous or broadleaf evergreens). Climate dictates, through hardiness and availability, the possibilities of mixing plants within a particular composition. Greater choice of broadleaf evergreen material is possible in warm climates and they may largely dominate a composition. In cold areas the deciduous materials will dominate, and the evergreens will be principally coniferous. Only rarely should any design composition consist totally of evergreen or deciduous plants instead of a mix of both. If costs must be kept to a minimum, deciduous materials are less expensive and create a mature composition sooner since they grow faster.

Leaf color can provide interest to plant masses. The transitions can be very subtle, as we discussed in regard to plant texture, or the color of individual plants can stand out as a point of emphasis. A plant like Japanese red maple (*Acer palmatum* var. *atropurpureum*) has a dramatic enough leaf color to become a simple specimen in a plant mass, thus serving as a focal point.

Through careful selection of plants it is possible to plan for flower color that changes in sequence between the individual plants of a large deciduous plant mass. Flowering will begin in early spring, to continue most of the season, perhaps to terminate in the fall with the bright crimson coloring of the leaves of winged euonymus (*Euonymus alatus*).

Scale. More variety and less repetition can be used in a small-scale design (such as a residential garden) in contrast to a large-scale design (such as an urban park), by using smaller masses of plants. The design effects must always be considered in relation to the scale or size of the area. In small-scale areas the viewing distance is short, and perception is thus changed considerably. Greater detail in individual plants can be observed at close range in small-scale designs. Subtleties in the changes of the color of leaves and flowers can be observed. Individual plants form masses in and of themselves in small areas where repetition can easily lead to monotony. Some people find that plants that are

25

too large become overpowering. This is especially true of shrubs planted in small areas. This would not necessarily include trees that rise above a person to provide shade and shelter, which are therefore welcomed as protection. Plant fragrances are more important in small areas than in large areas, because people can detect and enjoy the fragrances that are close at hand.

Some Design Problems. A designer must learn to anticipate possible problems and to devise a landscape to eliminate them. Many problems can be solved through a wise selection of plants.

Designers usually prepare a plan based upon the average mature growth of plantings. This can create problems when, for instance, the designer specifies a shade-requiring ground cover such as pachysandra under what will eventually be a large shade tree. Although in a few years it will provide the needed shade, the tree, when installed, is too small to provide the shade needed for the ground cover.

In the early years of many projects, sun-loving shrubs grow well and look good, but as trees provide increasing shade, they become spindly, thin, and unsightly.

Most people select plants that are potentially much too large for the spaces they must occupy. After a few years, increasing maintenance is needed as pruning becomes necessary. In many cases the plant crowds a sidewalk or patio and makes the use of these uncomfortable or difficult.

Generally, most clients want immediate results from plants. They are reluctant to wait several years for the landscape design to mature, and thus the designer is forced to place plants closer together on his plan than his experience tells him is wise. The design looks mature sooner, but the longevity of the plants is shortened. The plants will have to be replaced sooner because of initial close spacing.

Maintenance becomes a problem when ground covers have been planted among roses or other shrubs. Maintenance workers find that pulling weeds is a painful and frustrating experience.

Narrow or crowded spaces and unsightly surfaces can be a problem. Vines can be considered for these, especially where a plant is wanted that will be leafy to a great height, such as against a tall building alongside which a sidewalk has left a narrow planting space. Vines will also climb unsightly power poles and television towers. Wire fences can also be covered by vines, and the designer can make good use of changes in color and texture with vines by using Boston ivy (*Parthenocissus tricuspidata*) on a light brick or stone wall. When space allows, a facing of junipers will provide additional contrast with color and texture. Shade can be created in a limited space by directing vines over garden structures, porches, and so forth.

Grass will not survive when beech trees and other trees that have low spreading branches are planted in open lawns. Sparsely leaved and high-branching trees like thornless honey locust (*Gleditsia triacanthos* var. *inermis*) are more desirable where a luxuriant lawn is wanted, because they let more light filter through to the grass below. In southern California, Hawaii, and Florida palm trees are well suited were light shade is needed.

Consideration of color contrast is needed when designing for planting against walls and fences. Yews will not show up nearly as well against red brick as they will against a wall made of buff brick or white cast stone. A silver of blue juniper will provide better color contrast against the red brick.

Some trees are notorious for their surface roots, which are especially troublesome in heavy clay soils. When planted too close to paving, these roots will eventually heave the paving upward.

SUMMARY

The designer must be constantly sensitive to all the complexities of plants, both functional and aesthetic, that may affect the results of his design efforts. The success of a designer's work of art is dependent on his mastery of all the physical and environmental factors that are present, but it is also dependent on the quality of the construction and maintenance that follows the design. If the landscape designer is retained by the client to provide observation during construction, the quality of the use of lines, textures, color contrasts, repetition, variety, and emphasis can be achieved to the best advantage. The effect of the aesthetic elements is apt to fall short of expectations if the designer is not consulted about the maintenance of materials he has specified. Dead plants might be replaced with substitutions of other species that have a different form or color or texture, and the substitution would completely change the designer's composition. Thoughtless pruning may affect his composition as well. For instance, if the maintenance supervisor prunes individual privet and yew

2.51 A carefully designed curvilinear entrance road and informal planting provide both interest and visual privacy for a residential estate in Indiana.

plants in the form of square boxes in an otherwise informal planting design, the harmony of plant forms is destroyed in the composition.

The quality of the landscape can be improved when the landscape contractor and landscape maintenance supervisor both understand thoroughly the basic principles of design. But there is also need for the designer to understand construction and maintenance problems thoroughly, and these are described elsewhere in this book.

3

Functional Uses of Plants

Plants have many functional uses which extend far beyond the term "ornamentals" which is commonly applied to them. The control of glare, physical barriers to control pedestrian traffic, and ground covers to reduce soil erosion are just a few of these functional uses described in this chapter. Many of these functions will improve the quality of the environment as well as serving an aesthetic function or add "beauty" to a particular site.

VISUAL CONTROL.

Plants are used in highway medium strips and along highway edges particularly on curves where they can help reduce the glare of oncoming headlights. In this role they also serve for the visual or aesthetic improvement of the highway landscape. Roadside plantings are also very helpful to separate the light of highway traffic from adjacent residential areas, and in such situations many home owners can feel a sense of privacy and separation from the adjacent highway.

Visual barriers can be created to screen such objectionable views as an auto junkyard or a gravel pit. Plants may also be so arranged that they can direct the viewer toward and enframe a particularly desirable view from a highway, along a hiking trail in a park, or any other type of location.

There are two types of light which can be reduced by the careful use of landscape plantings. The first is "glare" which is the direct light from the sun or from any artificial source such as street lights or auto headlights. The second type is reflected light which is that indirect light bounced off from another surface, which is usually light colored. It may also be referred to as secondary glare. This is a particular problem in developed areas where there is extensive use of glass, white walls or light colored paving. Reflection is also a problem for those developments located near water such as lakes or oceans, beaches, and also in the northern climates where there may be considerable snow cover.

Plantings can be very effectively used to reduce both glare and reflected light. Thick plantings will provide the greatest blockage of oncoming light but sometimes might not be the most aesthetically attractive, thus, a mix of plantings may be more desirable in order to achieve a combination of functions. Plants which are placed too close to such light sources as street lighting or security lighting around buildings may be subject to excessive pruning by unskilled workers who may destroy the natural beauty of the plant, and even create problems with some species dying from attacks by insects and disease.

Reflected light can be blocked from making itself uncomfortable for the viewer by the placement of plants or trees against vertical reflective surfaces such as buildings. Large trees can be planted in paved areas to shade the paving and preventing the reflection of light from its surface. Designers will need to be

3.1

3.1 Plants can be used as a visual screen against moving lights on a road for the comfort of residents who live on the other side.

3.2 A median planting reduces the glare of oncoming headlight.

3.3, 3.4 Plants of varying heights and placement can control the brightness of both daytime light, which changes through the day as the sun changes and nighttime glare from stationary artificial lights.

3.2

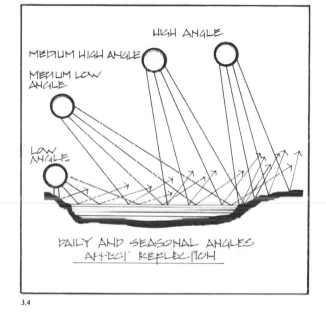

HIGH ANGLE

MEDIUM HIGH ANGLE

MEDIUM LOW ANGLE

LOW ANGLE

DAILY AND SEASONAL ANGLES AFFECT REFLECTION

3.4

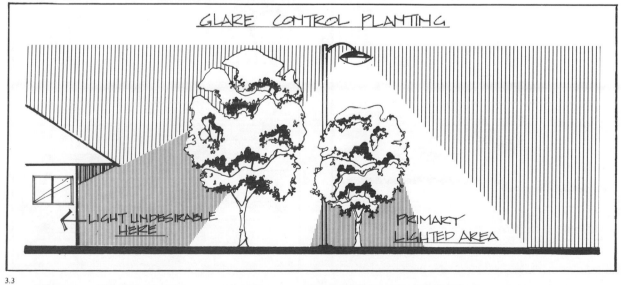

GLARE CONTROL PLANTING

LIGHT UNDESIRABLE HERE

PRIMARY LIGHTED AREA

3.3

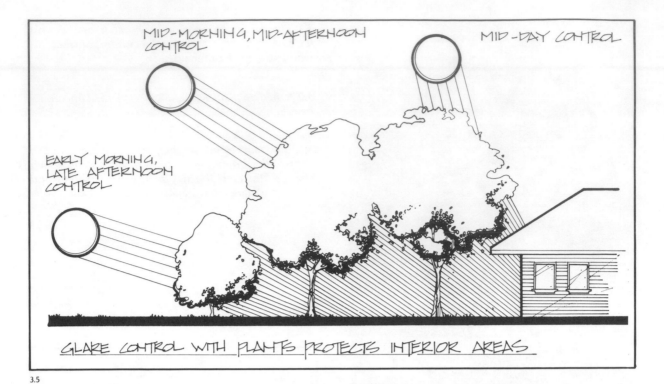

MID-MORNING, MID-AFTERNOON CONTROL

MID-DAY CONTROL

EARLY MORNING, LATE AFTERNOON CONTROL

GLARE CONTROL WITH PLANTS PROTECTS INTERIOR AREAS

3.5

3.5 Sun angles change seasonally, relative to Earth, thus changing the amounts of angles of glare.

3.6 Plants are effective in screening glare from adjacent surfaces such as water when the sun is low.

3.7, 3.8 Trees of varying heights help reduce glare from paving and building surfaces, making travel by foot or in vehicles more comfortable.

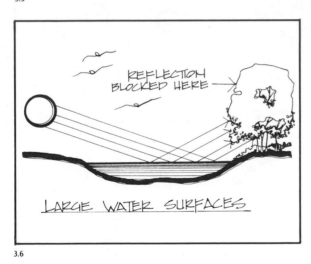

REFLECTION BLOCKED HERE

LARGE WATER SURFACES

3.6

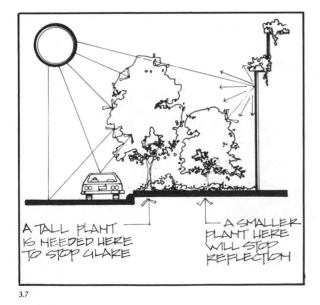

A TALL PLANT IS NEEDED HERE TO STOP GLARE

A SMALLER PLANT HERE WILL STOP REFLECTION

3.7

3.8

3.9

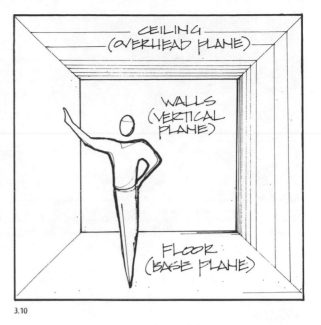

3.10

3.9 *Tall trees block reflection from a white wall.*

3.10 *The kind of space created by plants.*

familiar with the changing angle of the sun during the day as well as the seasonal changes in order to properly place plants for their maximum efficiency in reducing glare and reflected light.

In the area of visual control, plants may also be used as a form of architecture with the creation of outdoor rooms. Walls, ceilings and floors can be created with the effective use of plants. Hedges can be considered a wall of plants. A ceiling may be achieved when large shade trees are grouped closed together to create a canopy, or an overhead open wood structure covered with vines will create a similar affect. Grass and other combinations of low-growing plants commonly called ground covers serve as floors. As you may be able to see, there are many ways in which plants can be used to create and articulate various kinds of space and serve in different design functions. However, with plants there is not an immediate completed result. There is a time lag between the execution of the design and the time required for the plants to grow to maturity whereas when you build a building, the results are immediate.

Plants are an important consideration for the creation of privacy in residential areas where homes are placed close together. Although fences or walls do provide complete privacy in some situations, plants are a more pleasant and aesthetic addition. A combination of fences and plantings can provide the best of both worlds – the fence for immediate creation of privacy while the planting will add aesthetic qualities as they grow. For those with patience, small plants can be used as hedges, and these will ultimately create a solid visual screen at relatively low cost.

Plantings can be used to screen objectional views that occur around residential subdivisions, commercial, and industrial areas. These include trash receptacles, parking areas, electrical transformers, gas meters and valve stations, and storage facilities for vehicles, equipment and supplies. All of these functions require the careful and proper selection and placement of plants. Typically, plantings which are to be used for screens will need to reach six feet or more in height. If year-round screening is important, evergreen materials will need to be considered. Care should be taken to ensure that plantings will not be visually monotonous. Species should vary in texture, color and size as discussed later in this book.

3.11

3.12

3.11, 3.12 Plants define and enclose an area, creating an outdoor room.

3.13 Planted terraces enclose and define this outdoor space in Atlanta, Georgia.

3.14 Outdoor sculpture usually dominates nearby plantings. The plantings can be used to provide a setting for the sculpture so that it is the focal point of a space. This ten foot high sculpture of 6" x 6" timbers was designed and built by the author for his own residential landscape.

3.14

3.13

33

3.15

3.16

3.15 Plants help to define and create space or in some cases rooms with walls and ceilings. El Cajon Civic Center, California.

3.16, 3.17 Plants form a solid green wall that enclose a sitting area at the National Arboretum in Washington, D.C., and at the Morton Arboretum near Chicago, Illinois.

3.17

3.18

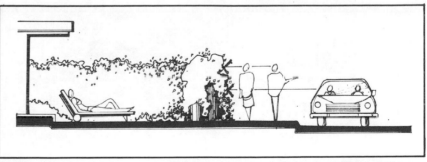

3.19

3.18 A canopy of closely spaced trees provides the sense of enclosure or room at this pedestrian plaza in Newport, California.

3.19 A residential living area can be made private from an adjacent street or other public areas through effective screen plantings.

3.20

3.21

3.20 *A recessed parking lot combined with planting provide complete visual separation of this parking area on the left from the residential area on the right. Museum of Art at Fort Worth, Texas.*

3.21 *Even in an arid environment such as Scottsdale, Arizona, planting can be used to screen parking lots.*

36

3.22

3.23

3.22 *Plantings separate a road on the right from the pedestrian walk in the center, bicycle lanes to the left and parking further to the left (which cannot be seen in this view). Harbor area near downtown San Diego.*

3.23 *Complete visual control will be achieved when this planting matures. Note the repetition of plant forms and the lines created that parallel the parking.*

3.24

PRIVACY VERTICALLY UPWARD TO ELEVATED ROAD OR WALK

PRIVACY CREATED BETWEEN BUILDING AND PLANTINGS

PLACEMENT OF LOW SHRUB VIEW NOT OBSTRUCTED

PRIVACY VERTICALLY DOWNWARD VIEW NOT OBSTRUCTED

3.25

3.24 Trees and shrubs form a screen to isolate a bicycle parking area from adjacent areas.

3.25 The effectiveness of plant screens for privacy will be affected by plant size in relation to terrain. Small plants will block a view uphill without obscuring a view from above. Taller plants may be needed for complete screening, and this may increase the time before the screen develops fully.

3.26

3.27

WORK AREA NOT VISIBLE FROM ABOVE

3.28

3.26 – 3.29 Plant screens block various objectional views: a service or utilities area, a construction equipment storage yard, junk pile, or sanitary land fill area and a quarry or mining area.

3.29

PHYSICAL BARRIERS.

The physical movement of people through certain landscape design situations can be effectively controlled with the use of plant materials. Low plantings of three feet or less may provide a more psychological type of control than physical though agressive individuals will certainly cross through and trample low plantings, especially ground covers. Children may find low planting very inviting to jump over as well as run through and in some situations plants need to be planted very close together and thorny varieties used in order to achieve any effective physical control. Those plantings which are three to six feet or more in height offer the greatest amount of physical control for both humans and animals.

Plants can be used as physical barriers along property lines and fences to divide certain sports activities within a park or to direct pedestrian traffic along various parts of a college campus. There are other possibilities that will emerge as each designer works to solve the problems of a particular project. As recommended with all uses of plants in various design situations, a variety of form, texture and color will be helpful to reduce monotony and increase aesthetic values.

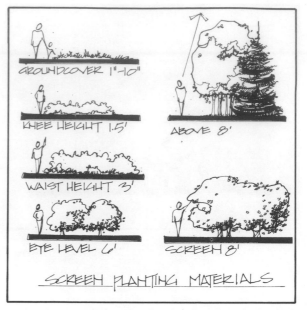

3.30 Selecting plants for visual control and physical barriers. Plant sizes affect spatial scale.

3.31 Small spaces may seem crowded if plants are installed that are eight or more feet tall. Conversely, an eight-foot plant in a large space may seem too small to achieve the necessary privacy. To a certain extent the sizes of the plants determine their functions.

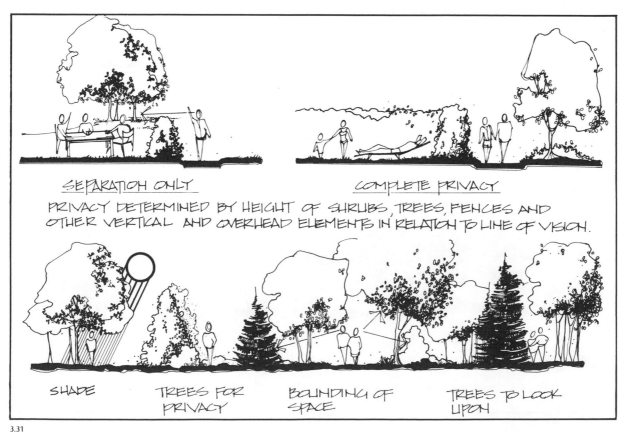

3.31

3.32

3.33

3.32 *A screened planting along the edge of a residential side yard for visual and privacy control.*

3.33 *A sitting area adjacent to a large office building. Privacy is achieved by a tall row of plants in the background which hide an adjacent parking lot.*

3.34 *The selection of plants to serve as physical barriers will depend on the use made of an area and the kind of control to be achieved. The lower panel summarizes the differences between psychological and physical barriers.*

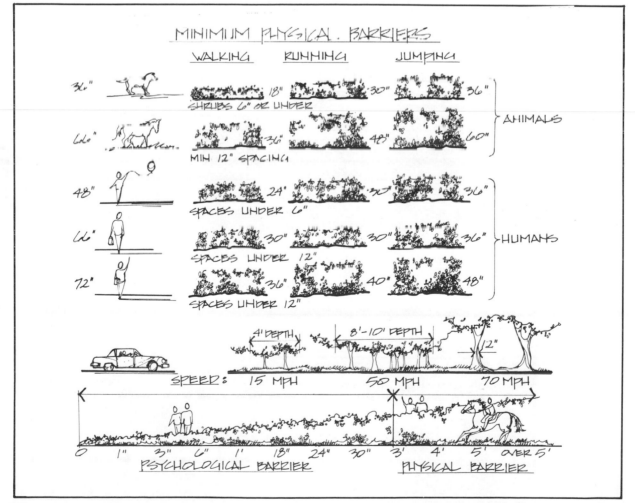

3.34

CLIMATE CONTROL.

The microclimate in a wide variety of situations, whether it is urban, suburban or rural, can be very effectively modified by the use of plants. Trees have provided shade and have been used for wind breaks for hundreds of years. The considerable use of asphalt and concrete in urban areas have had a dramatic effect on the rise of temperature levels. Plants can assist in reducing these temperature increases.

Comfort Zones. Human comfort should be a major concern of the designer and there are several climatic factors that affect human comfort. These are humidity, air temperature, air movement or wind, and solar radiation. In an accompanying illustration the "human comfort zone" is identified. When climatic conditions

3.35 The shaded area in the center of this diagram represents a climatic zone where temperature, humidity, wind, and solar radiation combine to provide the greatest human comfort. Bioclimatic data can be plotted in order to determine how corrective measures, such as windbreaks or canopy plantings, can be best implemented. The data will vary throughout the year as the climate of the region in which the site is located changes. Month by month there would be a little change in the bioclimatic data for Miami or Los Angeles and a great variation in the data for Minneapolis or New York.

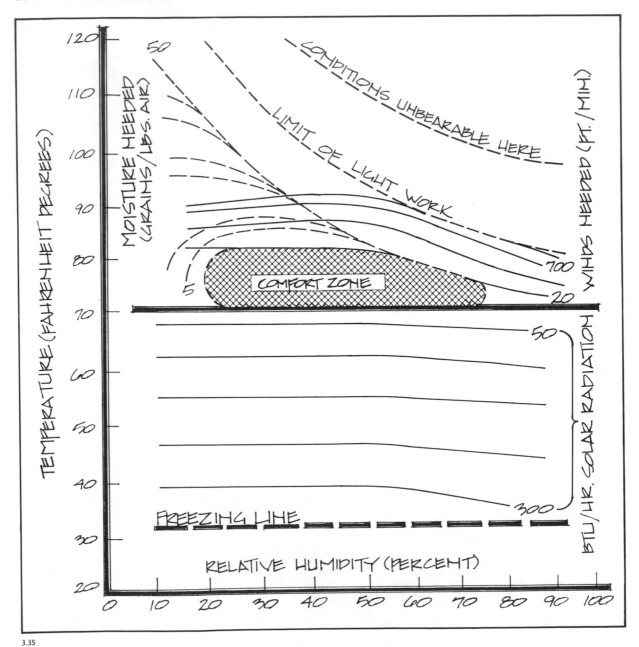

3.35

MORE SOLAR RADIATION
IS WANTED IN WINTER

3.36

PLANTS CONTROL SOLAR RADIATION

3.37

3.36, 3.37 Plants can obstruct and filter solar radiation or reduce its reflection. It is cooler beneath a plant that completely obstructs the radiation than it is beneath one that only filters it. Dark plants with small leaves will be effective in lessening the reflection of the radiation.

exceed the comfort zone then other remedies are desirable. One is the use of structures in which people live so they can escape the extremes through the use of heating or cooling. The other involves the use of plantings which can help at certain times to modify the climate and help restore the comfort conditions.

Solar Radiation and Temperature Control. Solar radiation is an important factor which affects our climate, but the amount of radiation received by the surface of the earth varies according to seasonal differences. There is more radiation in the summer when the sun is directly overhead than there is in the winter when it is lower on the horizon. There are daily variations, depending upon cloud cover which interferes with the amount of radiation reaching the earth's surface. The amount of radiation received by the earth's surface depends upon the nature of that surface. For instance, dark soils or asphalt paving absorb much of the radiation and retain heat which is then re-radiated back into the surrounding air. Light colored surfaces or light soils or sandy beaches reflect much of the radiation and quickly cool at night.

Vegetation in general reflects most of the incoming radiation. This coupled with the cooling effect caused by the transpiration of the leaves makes a significant difference in air temperature, which may be as great as 10 degrees F. lower in a heavily vegetated area such as a city park in contrast to a parking lot a block away. The temperature at night in a city can be five to ten degrees higher than in an adjacent rural farming area because of the re-radiation of heat from paving and building surfaces that have been absorbing it during the day.

Large trees can reduce the solar radiation that reaches a human and influence the comfort he/she experiences on a hot sunny day. Shade can have a dramatic affect on the comfort level. In the cooler season of the year such shade may not be welcome because it reduces the temperature below the comfort zone whereas standing in the sun may increase the feeling of comfort considerably.

The use of deciduous trees in cooler climates may serve a dual purpose by providing shade during the summer time and then allowing radiation to penetrate beneath them during the colder months. Air temperature and humidity might be in the right levels for human comfort but a steady severe wind can create an uncomfortable environment. In situations of prolonged high temperature and high humidity wind currents can be a welcome relief to reduce

43

the discomfort of the other two factors. It is the task of or challenge for the designer to study all of the factors involved in climate and use vegetation to either block or direct wind to achieve the greatest or maximum comfort level.

Planted windbreaks are well known for their effective control of wind. The amount of wind reduction is dependent upon the height, density, shape and width of these windbreaks. Height, however, is the most important consideration as it determines the size of the area adjacent to the windbreak where the greatest amount of protection is available.

A moderately dense barrier gives the greatest reduction in wind over the longest distance rather than a windbreak of higher density. Multiple rows of plants or trees usually provide the density required and have the lowest possibility of developing gaps due to a plant dying.

In areas where the movement of wind is desirable, plants can be used to direct the flow of air to that area. Because prevailing winds change directions seasonally there is a possibility that some wind screens can serve as a windbreak in the winter and then in the summer direct the breezes into the area where they are needed for summer cooling. When wind is directed into a narrow area like a funnel, the speed of the wind is accelerated and the cooling effect is increased.

A variety of color, texture and form in the selection of plants is desirable for the aesthetic appearance as well as to achieve the correct density in the planting. In most areas this would include the use of some evergreens.

CONTROL OF PRECIPITATION AND HUMIDITY

Plants add a considerable amount of water to the air through transpiration. The evaporation of this water contributes to some of the cooling effect felt underneath the shade of the tree. On a hot day 2,000 gallons of water can be transpired from an acre of forested land. The mulch that forms on the forest floor adds considerable humus which absorbs rainfall and helps retain water and prevent its runoff.

Precipitation control is also provided by plants in the control of snow movement. Row planting or windbreaks, as they were described earlier, can be also used to control the drifting of snow to keep it off driveways and sidewalks.

DENSE PLANTINGS CAN REDUCE WIND SPEED 75% TO 85%

3.38

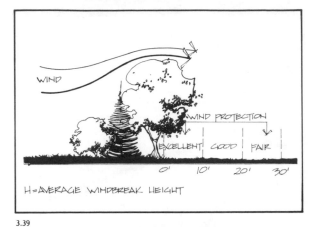

H=AVERAGE WINDBREAK HEIGHT

3.39

WIND FLOW

FOREST BLOCK

NARROW SHELTERBELT

WIND ABATEMENT BEHIND A FOREST BLOCK COMPARED WITH THAT LEEWARD OF AN EFFICIENT SHELTERBELT

3.40

3.38 Using plants for wind control: the arrows indicate wind direction; the undulating arrow denotes reduced wind velocity. The zone of greatest protection occurs where the people are standing. Height and penetrability of planting are more significant in reducing wind than the width of the plantings.

3.39 Areas of wind protection are related to the height of the planting.

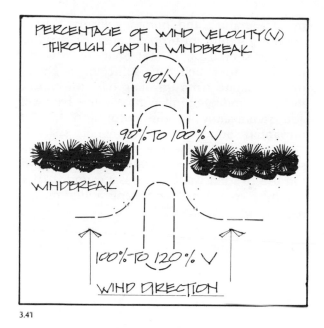

PERCENTAGE OF WIND VELOCITY (V) THROUGH GAP IN WINDBREAK

90% V

90% TO 100% V

WINDBREAK

100% TO 120% V

WIND DIRECTION

3.41

2 H

12 MPH   3 MPH

BARRIER WILL REDUCE WIND VELOCITY NEXT TO BUILDING

H = AVERAGE WINDBREAK HEIGHT

3.42

3.40 The arrows indicate maximum wind velocity. The largest area of protection occurs if a narrow shelterbelt is used, because much of the wind reduction caused by the forest block is measurable in the forest rather than beyond it.

3.41 A gap in a windbreak funnels the wind and increases its velocity.

3.42 Strategic location of plantings near buildings will control wind around and over them and may affect interior ventilation.

3.43 In areas where it is important to control snow drifting, the density of a windbreak will be important.

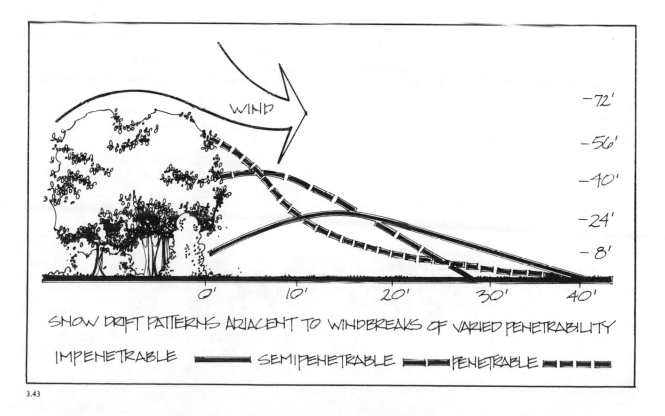

WIND

−72'
−56'
−40'
−24'
−8'

0'   10'   20'   30'   40'

SNOW DRIFT PATTERNS ADJACENT TO WINDBREAKS OF VARIED PENETRABILITY

IMPENETRABLE ━━━━ SEMIPENETRABLE ▬ ▬ ▬ PENETRABLE ▭ ▭ ▭ ▭

3.43

NOISE CONTROL

With increased urbanization and the use of motor vehicles, noise has become a problem of considerable concern in our outdoor environment. Architects have made progress in reducing noise within buildings by the use of materials that absorb unwanted sound. Some progress has been made in our urban areas by depressing freeways so that noise is absorbed by the slopes or radiated into the open atmosphere above the highway. Vegetation can help reduce outdoor noise and also psychologically separate the source of sound from the viewer.

Such things as walls or soil mounds in combination with plants will absorb or diffract sound waves as they come in contact with them. Soft objects such as leaves and soil tend to absorb the sound while hard objects such as smooth tree trunks and walls tend to deflect the sound and send the sound waves a different direction. Tall, dense evergreen plantings are more absorbent than other types but they must have their foliage to the ground in order to be effective sound barriers.

Noise is attenuated by distance. In other words, the loudness of noise is reduced the further you get away from it. Noise travel is also affected by wind direction and velocity as well as by temperature and humidity levels. Where noise is a significant problem areas devoted to planting should be 25 feet or more in width (more is better) and have sufficient height to prevent sound from traveling over the top of them. Mounding of soil in the planting base will add significantly to the absorption of the unwanted sound. In situations where space is very tight and sufficient distance from the source of the noise would be difficult to achieve the use of solid walls to act as a sound barrier could be considered, and plants added mostly for aesthetic purposes.

3.44 The effectiveness of sound control with plants will depend on the type, decibel level, intensity, and origin of the sound; the type, height, density, and location of the plantings and wind direction, wind velocity, temperature, and humidity. Some sounds may be louder and more irritating that others depending on a person's perception.

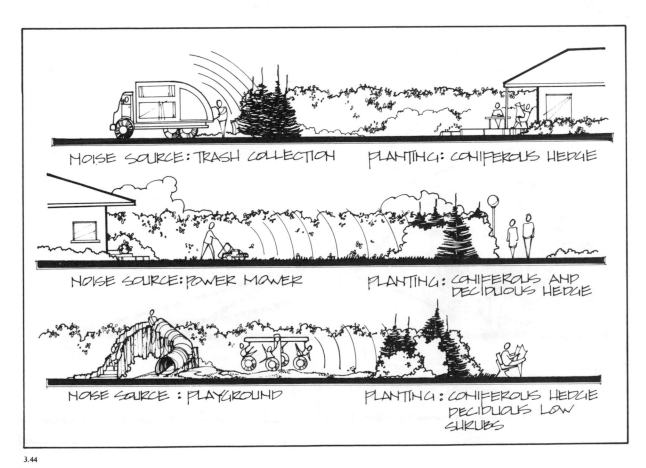

NOISE SOURCE: TRASH COLLECTION   PLANTING: CONIFEROUS HEDGE

NOISE SOURCE: POWER MOWER   PLANTING: CONIFEROUS AND DECIDUOUS HEDGE

NOISE SOURCE: PLAYGROUND   PLANTING: CONIFEROUS HEDGE DECIDUOUS LOW SHRUBS

3.44

3.45

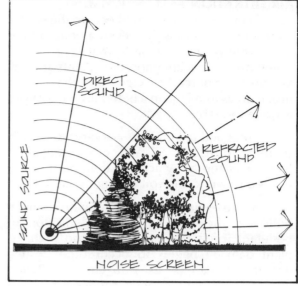

3.46

3.47

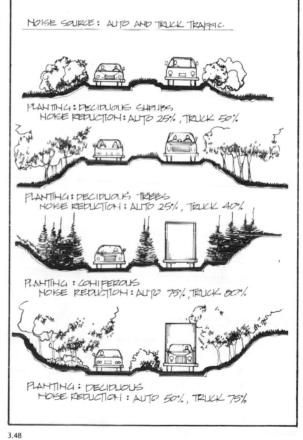

3.48

3.45 In flat terrain wide plantings in mounded strips are needed to provide satisfactory noise control.

3.46 Mixed plantings will give better sound attenuation than plantings of a single species. However, deciduous materials are not effective during the winter months.

3.47 A screen planting which separates a road from a residential area in Scottsdale, Arizona. The wall acts as an immediate visual and noise barrier until the planting can arrive at its maturity.

3.48 The shape of the terrain adjacent to a highway and the kind of plants installed there will influence the amount of noise control.

AIR FILTRATION AND ENRICHMENT

Plants act as "natural filters" in the earth's atmosphere. There is, however, a limit to their effectiveness and in industrial areas anti-pollution devices are important. Plants are well known as a source of oxygen and their use in urban areas to maintain a better level of oxygen is quite desirable.

Trees and taller plants are very affective in trapping dust, pollen and other sediments floating in the air which are then periodically washed down to the soil during precipitation.

Because plants will only tolerate so much pollution, they can be used as indicators of pollutant levels that are getting too high. As plant damage begins to occur other testing instruments can be used to check pollution levels to determine if they are indeed the cause of the plant damage.

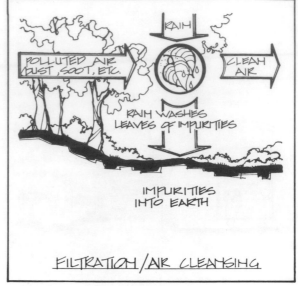

FILTRATION / AIR CLEANSING

3.49

REODORIZATION

3.50

EROSION CONTROL

Whenever the surface of the soil is disturbed either through construction activity or vehicular travel, or even foot traffic from human beings, erosion of the soil will occur. In agricultural areas where the soil is constantly tilled there is considerable erosion both from wind and rain and large amounts of top soil moves down the rivers and into the oceans each year. Soil erosion around our suburban and urban areas occurs every time construction activity begins.

Recreation areas are particularly susceptible to erosion damage. This can occur from the movement of people along hiking trails or any area that is subject to access by off-the-road vehicles.

To prevent and restore disturbed areas it is important that they be revegetated as quickly as possible. This may require the use of mulches or artificial mats or other means for holding the soil in place until the plants can re-establish themselves. In some cases irrigation systems may be required for a few years in order to provide the necessary moisture for plant growth. Where slopes or mounds are being used and a cover of grass is desirable, the use of sod rather than seed is a possible choice in order to achieve immediate cover and reduce soil erosion. When slopes are too steep, ground covers are more desirable because of the increased danger of mowing steep slopes. They also increase color and texture, and generally improve the aesthetic value of a particular project.

3.49, 3.50 Plants serve a function by filtering air and reodorizing air, and thus have an ability to lessen air pollution.

3.51 Many factors influence how extensively an area may be eroded. Plants are the best form of erosion control.

3.52 Plant qualities can lessen soil erosion. Horizontal branches prevent water from running down tree trunks to erode their bases; rough bark impedes water; leaves hold water and break the impact of raindrops; fibrous roots near the soil surface retain the soil; dense vegetation reduces areas of bare soil. A plant density that leaves two-inch bare spots between plants is not adequate protection against erosion.

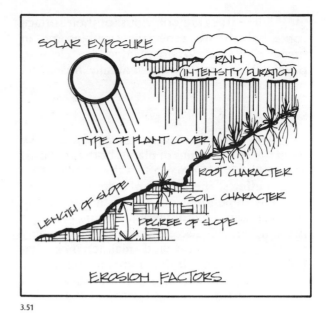

EROSION FACTORS

3.51

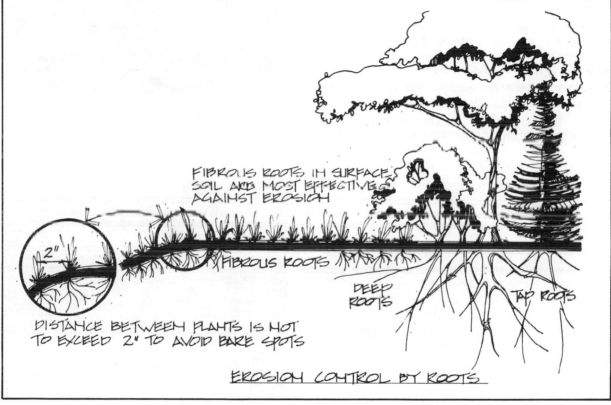

FIBROUS ROOTS IN SURFACE SOIL ARE MOST EFFECTIVE AGAINST EROSION

FIBROUS ROOTS

DEEP ROOTS

TAP ROOTS

2"

DISTANCE BETWEEN PLANTS IS NOT TO EXCEED 2" TO AVOID BARE SPOTS

EROSION CONTROL BY ROOTS

3.52

Some trees are notorious for their surface roots, which are especially troublesome in heavy clay soils. When planted too close to paving, these roots will eventually heave the paving upward.

SUMMARY

The designer must be constantly sensitive to all the complexities of plants, both functional and aesthetic, that may affect the results of his design efforts. The success of a designer's work of art is dependent on his mastery of all the physical and environmental factors that are present, but it is also dependent on the quality of the construction and maintenance that follows the design. If the landscape designer is retained by the client to provide observation during construction, the quality of the use of lines, textures, color, contrasts, repetition, variety, and emphasis can be achieved to the best advantage. The effect of the aesthetic elements is apt to fall short of expectations if the designer is not consulted about the maintenance of materials he has specified. Dead plants might be replaced with substitutions of other species that have a different form or color or texture, and the substitution would completely change the designer's composition. Thoughtless pruning may affect his composition as well. For instance, if the maintenance supervisor prunes individual privet and yew plants in the form of square boxes in an otherwise informal planting design, the harmony of plant forms is destroyed in the composition.

The quality of the landscape can be improved when the landscape contractor and landscape maintenance supervisor both understand thoroughly the basic principles of design. But there is also need for the designer to understand construction and maintenance problems thoroughly, and these are described elsewhere in this book.

3.53

3.53 The use of railroad ties (and planting to soften the appearance of the ties) is used to stabilize this sandy bank on the edge of Lake Michigan.

3.54 Concentrated use of this hiking trail along the top of a ridge in an Indiana nature preserve swept the litter away, exposing the soil to erosion during wind and rain storms. Exposed roots indicate the depth of the erosion.

3.54

4

Aesthetic Values

As spring emerges each year large numbers of people flock from their homes to the parks and forests to see the wildflowers and the new leaves that are beginning to emerge on the trees. This annual homage to the beautiful displays of nature illustrates the attraction that plants hold in the life of man.

It is a refreshing respite from winter for a homeowner to discover the crocus appearing in the garden and coming into blossom, to be followed by yellow forsythia and then a multitude of other blossoms in subsequent weeks. This fascination with plant color may wane somewhat during the heat of the summer, but as the leaves are suffused with the fiery colors of autumn the color-watch is renewed and man enjoys one last period of refreshment before winter returns.

Aesthetic values are generated not only from each individual plant, but also from the combination of such elements of the landscape as earth mounds and rolling topography. Masses of plants arranged in freeform, circular, and flowing patterns on similar forms of slopes and grades create a beauty that is unsurpassed. Some of these same aesthetic patterns occur in nature, where well worn or partially exposed rock outcroppings may alternate with wildflowers and tree masses, adjacent to a grassy meadow or surrounding a sparkling, clear lake with an undulating shoreline.

Changes in topography, in conjunction with changes in the height of plant masses, will create dimensional variations in the landscape, and most people find this pleasing. Few enjoy flat terrain if it is used monotonously. Designers are increasingly using earth mounds or land-sculpture to heighten the awareness of dimension in their planting designs. Other varietal changes can be achieved through the use of walls, fences, benches, and planters, in combination with plants. The hard materials provide immediate, permanent results while the plants modify and enhance the aesthetic values through their continuous growth and seasonal variety.

Moreover, in any well-designed landscape, harmonious relationships will be discernible between the colors, textures, forms, and lines of paving materials, structures, walls, etc., that the designer has used. The aesthetic values complement each other and convey a feeling of well-being and order.

Plants reflected in pools and ponds create patterns of light and shadow. Dark foliage creates a contrasting background for the white of a foaming fountain jet that shoots water several feet upward.

Shadows of plants create patterns of beauty on paving and walls, and these change by the hour as the Earth rotates. Patterns in the

4.1

4.1 *The light-green foliage of Quaking Aspen in the springtime contrasts against the deep blue skies along this high mountain road in the Wasatch mountains in Utah.*

4.2 The light colored grass is reflected by the clear water in a mountain stream on the Island of Maui, Hawaii.

4.3 Clear, sparkling cold water cascades from a spring and passes through a bed of watercress at the Cascade Springs in the Uintah National Forest of Utah.

summer will have sharp contrast with the bright sunlight, but the bare branches of winter will create intricate, more subtle patterns.

A unique kind of animation is expressed by plants as they respond to the wind. The slender, hanging branches of a weeping willow sway in a graceful way as the wind moves through them. The leaves of the quaking aspen shimmer or flutter even in a slight breeze.

When a wet snow falls in winter in neat little mounds on the branches of plants with dark bark, contrasting texture and new, unusual forms create a memorable beauty that occurs infrequently and disappears quickly.

The form of a large sycamore with patches of peeling bark is very majestic against a clear blue winter sky. Color is available during winter also from those plants that manage to retain their fruit. Some broadleaf evergreens turn from green to red or purple, providing other color changes. Plants provide the best color and textural relief to the drabness and monotony of winter.

4.3

Aesthetic values can be found in plant parts. Texture, color, and a feeling of design movement show in a wide variety of bark. The swirling patterns of knots are another element of design. Leaves provide a wide variety of forms and shape, most of them symmetrical in character. Subtle color changes and patterns are created by leaf veins. Some leaves are green above and powdery white below. Vivid color is provided by some, such as the Japanese red maple. When the sugar maple forests acquire their rich, warm autumn colors, few people can remain unmoved by the beauty.

Man has found it very difficult to duplicate the subtleties of colors and textures of flowers. Writers, poets, and artists over the ages have been enthralled with the beauty of flowers and have attempted to portray this beauty in a variety of ways. Firsthand contact with plants and their beauties is far superior to any written description or photograph.

The most successful functional and aesthetic uses of plants in design come about when the designer fully understands plants, their environments, and construction and maintenance problems. His efforts must then be followed by those of contractors who can faithfully install the materials according to plan and will freely communicate with the designer; finally, further work is needed by a maintenance supervisor who can understand the intent of the designer and who will care for, prune, and replace plants according to the design. If any one of this three-member team goes his own way without regard for the others, the functional and aesthetic values may be partially or even totally lost.

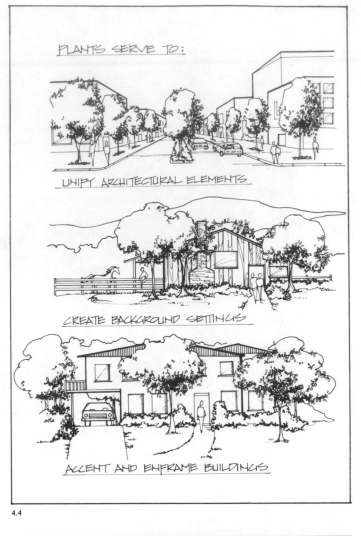

4.4

4.4 OFten the aesthetic effectiveness of plantings is dependent on the skill with which they are used in conjunction with architecture.

4.5 Plant materials, the unity of materials, and the paving and planters, waste containers, and drinking fountains, help to unify the architectural elements found in downtown Salt Lake City, Utah.

4.6 Plants provide a dark contrast to the white foaming fountain at the Indianapolis Museum of Art.

4.7 The planting provides a sense of enclosure as well as a backdrop for a fountain at the Chicago Botanical Gardens.

4.5

4.6

4.7

4.8

4.9

4.10

A. E. Bye and Associates

4.8 Trees, grass, flowers and water, all combine to make an attractive central courtyard for an office complex in Phoenix, Arizona.

4.9 A pleasant campus setting made possible with the use of plants and water. Richland College in Dallas, Texas.

4.10 The pattern of shadows of tree foliage, branches, and trunks on the paving surface and the green color of the leaves help relieve the starkness of a downtown area.

4.11 At the entrance to the Fort Worth Museum of Art, the massing of plants and repetition of trees makes an inviting entry area.

4.11

4.12

4.13

4.14

4.15

4.16

4.12-4.33 *A landscape architect needs to be aware of the aesthetic qualities of plant parts and plant settings that make each plant unique.*

4.12 *Leaves of the thornless honey-locust (Gleditsia triachantos 'inermis').*

4.13 *Leaves of the Japanese maple (Acer palmatum atropurpureum).*

4.14 *Newly emerging candles on the Scots pine (Pinus sylvestris).*

4.15 *Leaves of the sugar maple (Acer saccharum).*

4.16 *Foliage of the Norfolk Island pine (Araucaria excelsa).*

4.17

4.18

4.19

4.20

4.17 Individual leaf forms and character can be contrasted against the sky for plants such as the Japanese Maple (Acer palmatum).

4.18 These leaves feature a very coarse texture and high contrast from the light edges of the leaf to the dark green veins in the center.

4.19 Leaves have a certain translucency when viewed from below with the sun shining through them. This contrast against a dark background provides considerable interest to the viewer.

4.20 On the volcanic slopes of Hawaii, this grass is newly established and its light foliage stands in strong contrast to the dark lava.

4.21 Flower stalks of grass contrasting strongly against the dark blue of the sky in the background.

4.21

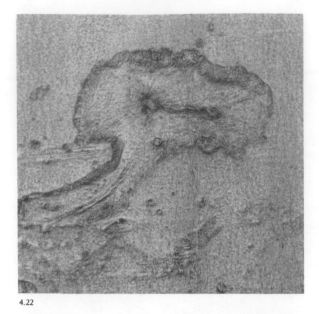

4.22

4.23

4.24

4.25

4.26

4.22 *The smooth, blotched bark of the American beech* (Fagus grandifolia).

4.23 *Interesting branch and bark patterns on a Fagus sp.*

4.24 *Exfoliation creates texture and color in the bark of the sycamore, or American planetree* (Plantanus occidentalis).

4.25 *Similar pattern created in another species of tree.*

4.26 *Trees silhouetted against the setting sun along the east shore of Lake Michigan.*

4.27

4.29

4.28

4.27 Fluffy-white clouds provide an interesting background in a desert summer sky in contrast to the Mexican Fan Palm.

4.28 A new, wet snow completely changes the character of plants in the wintertime, but the effect, of course, is only temporary.

4.29 Snow adds an additional contrast and interest in the wintertime to the dark branches of this Sasafras sp.

4.30 Frost gathering on these branches offer a strong contrast to the dark of the water in the adjacent stream.

4.30

4.31

4.31 The lotus blossom stands in soft and subtle contrast against the adjacent foliage. (see front cover)

4.32 Flowers of the Ranunculus sp.

4.33 Flowers of Clematis sp. *stands out in bold contrast to its darker foliage.*

4.32

4.33

5

Process of Planting Design

SITE ANALYSIS

The process of making a planting design, as practiced by the designer, is a very systematic one. After determining particular, unique needs and wants of the client, the designer must make a very thorough analysis of the site. It may be a site that the designer is already quite familiar with, if previously he prepared a master plan for the location of buildings, roads, parking areas, walks, patios, or other things, and the planting plan may be only a concluding phase of his work. In other projects an architect or engineer will have done the earlier planning of the site, leaving consideration of the landscape architect or designer until last. This working arrangement is less desirable because a number of mistakes may have been made that will affect the final aesthetic qualities of the site. Insufficient spaces may be left for planting, inadequate soil qualities may be on hand, or drainage may not have been anticipated.

A thorough site analysis should include, at least, the following:

1. Development of a site plan or plot plan showing the location of all structures and physical features, such as roads, walks, fences, walls, lakes, existing trees, and rock outcroppings. Utilities should also be located, both above and below the ground. Topographic characteristics that define warm and cold slopes, exposed and shaded areas, etc., are useful. The site plan should also show drainage patterns on the surface and notations about subsurface drainage and depth of the water table.

2. Determination of soil characteristics, such as soil pH, fertility, humus content, and compactability. On large site soils may change drastically from one part of the site to another. One part of the site may be in a flood plain with a high water table, but another part may be an upper plateau with good drainage. Still another area may have a clay soil with good surface drainage but little permeability.

3. Climatic characteristics. The relation of the site to the total region needs to be studied. Cold-hardiness zone maps are generally helpful for such study. Microclimatic characteristics close to the site should be studied. Information about such factors as average temperature and rainfall can be secured from local meteorologists, but it is also useful to determine whether the site is exposed to prevailing winds or protected from them, and to determine the direction and intensity of these winds. Whether part or all of the site faces north or south will be important in determining what hardiness to plan for in plants. The choice of low plants and ground covers in some areas will be affected by the potential depth of the snow cover during the coldest portions of each winter. Some regions can expect a consistent cover of several inches of snow, but others may experience little or no snow, winter after

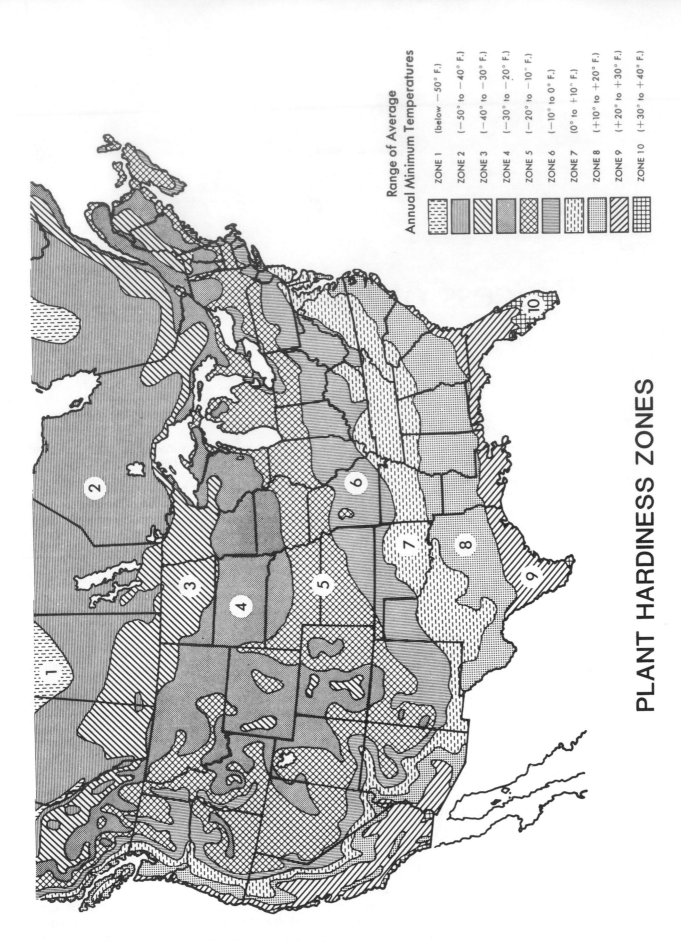

PLANT HARDINESS ZONES

5.1 A map of the zones for plant hardiness established by the U.S. Department of Agriculture.

winter. Less-hardy species will endure if they are protected by a consistent snow cover.

4. Functional and circulation characteristics. If the site is unoccupied at the time the site analysis is made, many of these characteristics must be determined with the help of the client or else estimated. For sites in use, observation of vehicular and pedestrian circulation patterns over a period of time will help to ensure that potential plant locations are given the most efficient, functional uses. Other functional locations may be determined by standard practice; for instance, large trees are not compatible on the south and west sides of swimming pools and tennis courts, because leaf, flower and seed litter in pools will result, and distracting shadow patterns on the courts will be caused.

5. Aesthetic factors. Determine the location of good views, and also the location of poor views that may require screening. It is always good to consult with the client about these. A client may prefer one view instead of another for the reasons a designer cannot anticipate, and his personal likes and dislikes may require the designer to develop unique solutions because of a client's personal objections to neighbors or objects and structures on adjacent properties. For the most part, however, the designer's personal taste and judgment play a predominant role in evaluating the aesthetic characteristics of a site. Because of his training and experience, a designer will be capable of making judgments that will prove satisfactory to a majority of clients, most of whom will not be able to express why they like what they see but will admit they find if pleasant and enjoyable.

PLANT SELECTION

The effective use of plants in design requires a personal acquaintance with them. This can be done in several ways.

1. Take a course in school where each student is physically introduced to one plant at a time and memorizes its characteristics (as well as assembling a set of notes for future reference which could include pencil sketches and photographs).

2. Consult a computer data base or better, prepare one from notes assembled from No. 1 above. A computer facilitates rapid selection of plants from a wide range of criteria and provides the designer a broader pallette of plants than time would normally allow. A description of one such data base and software appears in Appendix 5–A at the end of this chapter.

3. Acquire reference books on plant materials such as those listed in Appendix 5–B at the end of this chapter. These can also be used to help build a computer data base.

4. Secure nursery catalogs and inventory listings from state nursery associations to determine availability of the plants you want to use. This information could also be added to your computer data base. A list of state nursery associations can be found in Appendix 5–C.

Having thoroughly analyzed the site, the designer begins the process of assembling a list of plants compatible with the findings of his site analysis. Other factors will also influence this selection. The availablity of plants from established nursery sources is important. There is little value to selecting and using a plant in a planting plan if the landscape contractor finds it cannot be obtained. Whether or not good maintenance is available to the client will also influence plant selection. Those plants requiring extensive annual pruning and pest control will have to be minimized or eliminated from the design if good maintenance is not available. In nearly every project, cost becomes important and most clients are reluctant to plan for expensive maintenance, so the designer may have to select plants that require little maintenance to reduce cost. All clients should be persuaded to understand that some maintenance and some cost is necessary even when a project has been most carefully designed and planned to minimize it.

Occasionally clients will browse through a nursery catalog and ask the designer, "Can I have a plant like this one?" Usually they are attracted by the color of the flowers. Rarely do they understand that the plant must have some relationship to the total design. The plant they have seen in the catalog may not be hardy, or it may not be adaptable to the soils on the client's site. It then becomes the educational task of the designer to describe some basic principles of plant ecology, or to show a client plant examples already growing in the area of his site, and to orient him to the nature of design. This procedure may be needed more often in dealing with a residential client than with corporate or institutional clients, who may be quite accustomed to leaving all details of a delegated job to the professional they have engaged.

Dislikes of some plants will arise generally from unpleasant experiences. A child, having fallen into a clump of roses or a barberry bush, may dislike such plants permanently. It is always good to determine if a client has a dislike of some plant the designer plans to use. Some education of the client in the qualities of disliked plants may or may not be helpful.

PLANT CHARACTERISTICS AS A DESIGN DETERMINANT

Once he has assembled a list of plants to be used for the design of a project and has taken into account the information gained from the site analysis, the design then considers the form, size, texture, and color of each plant to be used.

Form. There are a wide variety of forms. We mentioned the categories or horizontal and vertical forms earlier. These are the broadest categories. Trees and shrubs grow mainly in columnar, round or ellipsoidal, pyramidal, round-weeping or-drooping, and v- (or vase–) shaped forms. Some may have forms that combine these basic shapes. Horizontal form is characteristic of shrubs more than it is of trees, and some shrubs grow in horizontal-oval and mounded-to-flat form. Shrub forms may seem to hug the ground, whereas the forms of trees will be supported in the air on their trunks.

The vertical forms of individual plants will change to (or "read") as a horizontal form or unit when the plants are placed together in a group for a mass planting.

Prime consideration must be given to the form of a plant when it is used as an individual specimen for a focal point or for emphasis in a design composition. Individual forms become less noticeable when several plants are closely spaced; then the form of a plant is likely not to express itself well or at all. A ground cover is an example of which forms of the individual plants of the same species are lost as part of the whole mass. Care must be taken never to use too many different forms together; too much variety of form will create a "hodge-podge" rather than a designed composition with aesthetic value.

The form of deciduous materials may change somewhat during the changing of the seasons. Where a strong oval form may be evident in a tree when foliage is luxuriant, only a very weak oval form will be perceived in winter, at which time the upright pattern of the branches of the center of the tree may be more dominant than the overall tree form observed in summer. Depending upon the circumstances, seasonal variations may have considerable effect on the design.

Size. What will be the ultimate or mature width and height of plants selected? Many plant listings or encyclopedias list these sizes. In most instances the sizes given are for full grown under ideal environmental conditions and may not represent growth potential of the site for which the design is being created. Therefore, the designer can find it helpful to consult with local nurserymen and horticulturists, and to rely on direct observation. Sometimes an accurate judgment of potential plant size is needed in conjunction with the spacing of plants. More will be said about size later in this chapter under "Spacing of Plants."

5.2 Some of the most common tree and shrub forms. Various combinations of each of these forms can be found and there is a variety of plant sizes within each form.

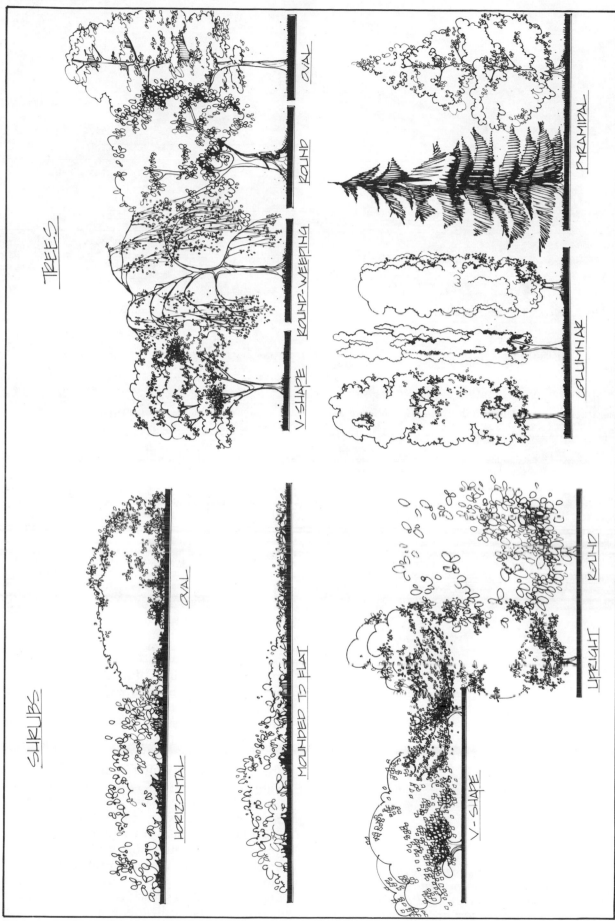

TREES

OVAL
ROUND
ROUND-WEEPING
V-SHAPE
PYRAMIDAL
COLUMNAR

SHRUBS

OVAL
HORIZONTAL
MOUNDED TO FLAT
V-SHAPE
UPRIGHT
ROUND

5.2

5.3

A. E. Bye and Associates

Texture. The texture of each plant can be expressed in a number of ways. Texture varies also with the distance of the viewer from the plant and relates, usually by contrast, to adjacent textures. A plant with large leaves may express a coarse texture during summer, but in contrast to other plants during winter its branching pattern might be fine in texture. With some plants there is no difference. The large leaves of *Magnolia soulangeana* express a coarse texture and the bold branching pattern will also be coarse in winter. Tallhedge buckthorn (*Rhamnus frangula* var. *columnaris*) is coarser in texture during the summer than common privet (*Ligustrum vulgare*), which has small leaves, but their winter textures are practically identical.

5.3 *Skillful use of a variety of textures in a naturalistic project. An analysis of plant textures such as those shown in Chapter 2 was needed in planning this project. As a result, the textures combine naturally.*

Evergreens offer the advantage of consistent texture. Rhododendrons and yews are examples, respectively, of coarse and fine textures that will provide a year-round consistency in the design.

5.4 When flowers are used in landscape design they can add considerable interest and color.

Color. Flowers, fruit, leaves, and branches are all sources of color and are all influenced by seasonal variations. In general, flowers on trees and shrubs are short lived, though their visual effect can be quite dramatic. A mass of forsythia in bloom during spring is an example; it remains a popular plant though it offers little interest the remainder of the year.

Fruit value varies from plant to plant. Some fruit offers little contrast in color or showiness, but in other plants the fruit may be more dramatic than the flowers. If fruit color is dramatic or the fruit is persistent into fall and winter after the leaves have dropped, it becomes an important consideration in design. Pyrancanthas are just one of many examples of shrubs with colorful and persistent fruit; species of this genus have berrylike fruit ranging from yellow-orange to scarlet and crimson, colors much more important than the flower colors of the shrubs.

The light, fresh green color of new leaves in spring can offer refreshing design possibilities. A deep contrast can be seen between the dark green of the past year's needles and the light color of the coming year's new growth in yew shrubs. The same is true among most conifers. Japanese red maple (*Acer palmatum* var. *atropurpureum*), begins the year with pale red leaves, which darken to purple as spring changes to summer. Plants that possess a leaf color dramatically different from the usual variations of green are useful for accents and points of emphasis in a design composition. Moreover, they reduce monotony and create a pleasant variety. As is true in using any element of design, too much variety of color will cause a design to look confused and disorganized and will destroy an otherwise pleasant aesthetic effect.

The fall coloring of leaves should also receive consideration. Winged euonymus (*Euonymus alatus*) present an especially fiery display of color. This plant will always catch the eye and can easily occupy the center of a composition.

Branches are a useful source of winter color, though their color is apt to be less noticeable against the sky and thus can be given lower priority in a design than the other considerations just discussed. In a particular project, however, a plant such as red-osier dogwood (*Cornus stolonifera*), against a light grey fence, might become a central focal point in a garden during the winter. The dark brown branches of a nicely or artistically formed tree makes interest contrast against the light brick or white cast stone walls of large buildings.

SPACING OF PLANTS

As living things, plants vary in size according to age. This ever changing factor presents problems to the designer. Some clients want a landscape that will look mature as soon as it has been installed, and if they can afford it in their budget, large-sized plants can be selected that may be several years of age. The general tendency is to place young plants too close together, without anticipating the ultimate size of the plant.

The designer should learn to think in terms of three common categories of plant size. Besides knowing the nursery size, the size at which plants are commonly sold, the designer plans for their full size at maturity (or old age), but he also familiarizes himself with their

5.5 When plants are spaced close together so that their average mature forms touch, horizontal masses are then created. This is usually more attractive than spacing the plants so far apart that they never touch.

5.6 A flower border in front of a shrub-tree grouping adds additional interest on this campus of Brigham Young University.

"average" mature size. Full size will vary according to the planting location and soil factors. Under ideal site and soil conditions a particular tree may grow to a height of 100 feet, but the particular characteristics of a site may restrict its growth to an ultimate height of 60 feet. If the tree is planted in a raised, enclosed planting bed, this will restrict its ultimate height even more, and it will probably shorten the tree's life-span as well.

Generally, most designers will base the plant spacing on their plans according to the average mature growth of the plants, and can thus achieve a design that looks full and mature before the plants reach their ultimate maturity. In some projects it is best to space the plants very close together for immediate effect. Hedges and

5.6

privacy screens are examples of planting in which a dense appearance is so important that the designer may plan for close spacing even of young plants.

THE USE OF FLOWERS
IN PLANTING DESIGN

For the moment, let us confine our discussion to flowers such as perennials, annuals, and bulbs, instead of the flowers of trees, shrubs, or ground covers. Flowers require a great deal of maintenance, in return for which they provide considerable visual and aesthetic appeal, and most homeowners insist on providing some space for them in a garden

design. The smaller or reduced scale of the residential garden allows intimate contact with flowers, which can be manipulated frequently and freely and given a kind of care not needed for other plants. However, most corporate, institutional, and governmental clients will limit the use of flowers to areas of special interest or positions of maximum exposure, because of the cost of their maintenance.

Generally, flowers should be planted against a background of shrubs or along a fence. In a planting bed the lowest flowers should be placed in front, with one or more masses of flowers of increasing height behind them. Plants should be selected so that a sequence of flower color will continue throughout the season, but attention should be given to avoiding clashes between adjacent colors that do not harmonize.

71

THE DESIGN PROCESS

The actual process of making a planting design begins after much of the other planning of a project has taken place. First comes the site analysis, as we described earlier, which is followed by a master plan. Buildings are precisely located, then designed by an architect. The landscape architect prepares the site plans for roads, walks, plazas, fountains, steps, walls, etc., in cooperation with engineers who are handling several technical details, including the design of underground utilities. Even though the landscape architect has kept his planting design in mind during the entire planning process and has thought about preserving existing trees on the site, developing his grading plans to avoid disturbing them, he begins to develop his planting drawings near the end of his "planning." Ideally the planting plan and sprinkling plans are prepared simultaneously and closely coordinate. The engineers will need to know some details of the sprinkling plan when they design the water mains.

The trend in landscape-architectural offices today is toward multidisciplinary staffing, so that several specialists are brought together to work on one project. The most successful planting designs will be created when designers, plant specialists, and maintenance specialists work together in reaching design solutions. The aesthetic value of a design will be increased and maintenance costs will be reduced to a greater extent than when a project is designed by one individual.

Utilizing the most up-to-date site plans, the designer makes an ozalid print of the site plan, places the print on his drafting board, and covers it with a sheet of light-weight sketching tissue.

Elevations of nearby buildings and perspectives of portions of the site should be used for coordinated study with the plan.

Using a soft pencil, the designer begins to place plant masses on his tissue sketches of plans and elevations. During this sketching, plant names are not applied. The designer studies these masses for their contribution to the composition. He may need to adjust their placement for the best combination of emphasis, repetition, and balance. Next he will think about the textures he wants to create, sketching these with appropriately varied widths of vertical lines. At the same time, the designer studies use of form, line, and color, comparing various combinations of these in turn on the plan and on elevations. Names and individual locations for each plant are now determined from the list previously prepared. If significant changes in the details of the site plan were made after the plant list was prepared, a cross-check is advisable to make sure the plants selected earlier still fit the particular environmental conditions created by sun, shade or wind, etc., on the site. Three, four, or more studies will be made on the light-weight sketching tissue before the final solution has been determined.

The next step—preparation of plans and specifications—is discussed extensively in Chapters 6 and 7.

SOME GENERAL CONSIDERATIONS

In designing for plants, plants cannot be considered in and of themselves to the exclusion of all else. When they are placed on a site they can transform it, but it is important for the designer to remember that the site existed earlier, and its inherent or existing characteristics will control the success or failure of the finished site depending upon how well or how inadequately the designer understands and works with these characteristics.

A planting design for a large urban area dominated by buildings and paving can be bold and dramatic, but in rural, more natural settings, the design will need to be very subtle to fit into the existing landscape. In between these extremes is a wide variety of other sites requiring considerable intuitive ingenuity on the part of the designer before a design can be made that is satisfactory both functionally and aesthetically.

Some planting designs will have, as an important function, the remedy of bad site planning. Through lack of planning, many buildings are intrusions upon the natural landscape, poorly fitted to the site. The designer may be called upon to try to improve the site with the use of plants. Exposed foundations and crude grade-changes call for plant masses to create a smoother, more aesthetic transition from building to site. Tall buildings can be made to fit their surroundings by the use of tall trees. Large expanses of windowless walls can be broken visually with columnar trees planted close to the walls. Shrub masses are effective around smaller buildings, creating a sense of lengthened horizontal dimensions and pulling the structure closer to the ground visually.

5.7 *In a naturalistic style setting, this small recreation shelter seems quite at home.*

5.8

NATURALISTIC APPROACH TO DESIGN

Of increasing appeal to some people is the idea of a return to nature. To design landscapes that seem to have developed naturally requires a thorough knowledge of plant ecology. It also requires a tolerance by the client for a lack of neatness in the landscape, because a naturalistic design is not a manicured one. There is a vast difference between informal and naturalistic design. An informal design may make use of curved, irregular lines, but the finished appearance reveals attention to order and tidiness. However, in naturalistic design, such things as line, form, color, and texture appear only the way nature allows them. Only those plants that are compatible with each other and with the environmental conditions of the site are used, and these will survive without man's help.

As the naturalistic design matures, additional plants can be added. For instance, during maturity some areas of the site may have become shaded and the soil surface will have become built up with forest humus. Shade-loving ferns and wildflowers can be added where conditions have developed for which they are compatible.

5.9

5.8 This golf green was carefully sited for a natural backdrop of existing plants in the Rocky Mountains.

5.9 When this park and playground were designed the existing white pine in left center was saved and additional trees added for a park-like atmosphere.

5.10

5.11

DESIGN CONSIDERATIONS OF SOME PROJECTS

The following examples of design projects are not all-inclusive but are intended to provide a general introduction to the variety and particular characteristics of the design problems a practicing designer can expect to encounter. Our emphasis here is on ways all the design elements we have discussed are used in a variety of projects, without studying more than their design qualities.

Parks and Recreation Areas. The use of shrubs, especially large masses, is not often wise in urban parks, even though they might be desirable. In many parks it is necessary for civil authorities to monitor park activities to ensure the protection and safety of the people who use the park. Experience has shown that where shrub masses are used, even though they provide privacy, they also provide a screen for criminal activity. The designer may want to strive for the maximum amount of openness with his design.

Where the design of the park is informal, the tree planting should also express an informal quality. Random spacing and grouping of trees will yield the most successful results. In highly developed parks – those that are created largely out of architectural materials and in which the space for plants is minimal – the designer may have to use a different approach. Parks of this type are usually given a modular design utilizing straight lines. Tree plantings in such parks will be more effective if designed formally to harmonize with the rest of the park design.

Roof Planting. There is increasing use of planting on the tops of structures above, at, or below street level. These gardens, parks, plazas, or whatever they might be called, pose special problems. Because planting beds will be entirely surrounded by some kind of container, temperatures are likely to reach extremes that will affect the hardiness of plants used, root zones will be restricted, and patterns of light intensity and reflection, shade, and air movement may all be quite unusual.

Moreover, there are structural problems that the designer should consider. Few structures are designed to support the weight of soil in the quantities needed for a luxuriant landscape.

Trees will have to be planted in raised containers over the supporting columns of the structure. Some designers have arranged soil mounds over the columns and placed a boxed

5.10 Weeping willows have existed for many years along a pond in Boston Gardens and make a significant contribution to the park-like setting in this urban area.

5.11 Waterfront Park, a redevelopment project between downtown Boston and the waterfront. Planters can be used for color and plant materials in areas where it may be difficult to grow plants in-ground.

75

5.12 *In downtown North Canton, Ohio, a park adds considerable attractiveness to what might be a drab urban area.*

Photo by Donald A. Teal

5.13

5.16

5.14

5.15

5.13 *Planting as part of the New Orleans Zoo development.*

5.14 *Existing trees were carefully preserved in this golf course setting in the Rocky Mountains.*

5.15 *Attractive planting which enframes this entrance to a golf course club house.*

5.16 *A playground carefully designed into an existing park setting with existing trees in Akron, Ohio.*

5.17 Privacy and wind control are assured at this tennis court in Dallas, Texas.

5.18 Roof planting along a series of terraces that form the underground bookstore on the University of Minnesota's campus.

5.19, 5.20 Roof planting and reflection pond that form one of three similar roof terraces for a corporate headquarters in Connecticut.

tree at the center with an informal grouping of small shrubs on other portions of the mound, and ground covers the rest.

On large structures, grass may be usd to connect soil areas between supporting columns; for grass the soil layers can be thinner than for shrubs.

The availability of water and other utilities will limit what can be done. Consideration must be given to drainage and irrigation. Projects of this type that are actually parts of structures are usually heavily used areas and lighting is often needed so that the project can be used during evening and night hours. Carefully placed lights in concealed sources are successfully used and aesthetically pleasing. Designs of this kind are good places to make use of water, either in a splashing fountain or a reflection pool, both of which will enliven a small plaza without requiring a great amount of space.

78

5.19

5.20

5.21 *Addition of trees, planters and seating adds both visual interest and greenery to the urban desert. Akard Street Mall in Dallas, Texas.*

Urban Center Areas. Closely related to roof planting in several of its problems is "street scaping," or the revitalization of downtown areas, using plants as one of the components of this work. There are few streets in modern cities that do not have a multitude of utilities beneath the paving. Besides covering conduits for telephone and power cables, paving may have been laid over pipes for heating and cooling systems, water, and sanitary sewage and storm runoff systems. All combined, these can limit the amounts of soil available for the root zones of most plants. Securing sufficient information on underground utilities during site analysis is nearly always a problem inasmuch as few cities maintain adequate and accurate maps. Some

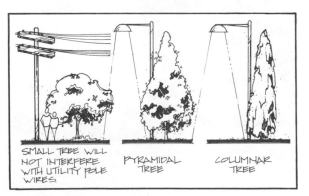

SMALL TREE WILL NOT INTERFERE WITH UTILITY POLE WIRES

PYRAMIDAL TREE

COLUMNAR TREE

5.22 *Street tree planting must be planned so as to avoid interference with power lines or light poles. Some trees are more suitable than others because of their shapes. Light poles that clear the foliage of the tree are desirable, too.*

5.23 Dry style landscaping for the Public Library at Sun
City West, Arizona.

5.24 Extensive planting that forms the entrance to the Fort Worth Museum of Art.

5.25

5.26

lines may have been installed privately without being placed on city maps. Quite often lines are changed during construction because of other hidden utilities or obstructions, thus making the city's drawings more inaccurate.

Designers often find raised planters convenient because these can be designed to provide sufficient surface soil space for planting. Irrigation in some form is generally a necessity.

Plant selection is crucial since the plants must tolerate air pollution, root restrictions, heat, cold, wind, and other rugged conditions not common in other projects for which plants are used.

Housing Developments. In designing plantings for a low-cost housing development, the designer's choices will be severely restricted by his budget. For this reason, unfortunately, planting is usually kept to a minimum. Because of cost limitations, most of the plants selected are small in size and of inexpensive, deciduous species. They must be capable of surviving with little or no maintenance. Trees usually must be planted so sparsely that locating them carefully in the composition is critical. Selection of very durable species is also important.

5.25 A landscaped pier near downtown San Diego.

5.26 Planting and decorative pool that are part of a motel development in Tucson, Arizona.

5.27 A housing development near Vail, Colorado, where the existing conifers and vegetation were allowed to remain.

5.28 A housing development which has been carefully sited and constructed into an existing wooded area leaving as many of the existing trees to remain as possible.

82

5.27

5.28

When a large budget is available, as it often is for high-quality condominium developments, the designer has greater freedom to produce a planting plan that is both functional and aesthetic. Large plants can be used for a more immediate result. The creation of outdoor living spaces and installation of plant masses to screen noise, hide objectionable views, and provide privacy are some of the things that can be more easily designed for a project if the budget is large.

Schools and Campuses. In the past decades of the 50s and 60s there was a surge of construction of educational facilities. Growth since then has slowed. Landscape architects have been involved in many phases of this work, including site selection, master planning, and site engineering, as well as planting design, with most of the work being done at new institutions of higher education, which often comprise several buildings on a campus. Elementary and secondary school districts have sought the services of landscape architects less frequently, relying instead on parent-teacher groups to provide the landscaping. This is especially true in rural areas.

There is about as much variety in planting design for schools as there are designers. Each school will have conditions that make a slightly different approach to arranging the plants necessary; many of the differences are dictated less by the site than by school-administrative preferences and cost factors. Because school buidings are large, designers will generally attempt to create a smaller, more human scale. If the shrub masses used are generally horizontal in character and are kept simple, this will make a large building seem lower. To complement the austere, geometric lines of modern architecture in a building with a large mass, large numbers of the same plant species can be used in continuous masses rather than smaller numbers of several species, as would be typical in a residential garden.

5.29 Housing development in Atlanta, Georgia, where extensive plantings were added to provide a green environment for the residents.

5.30 A parking lot in Atlanta, Georgia, was broken into small groupings with considerable planting to break up the asphalt desert.

5.31 In an existing wooded area the parking was carefully sited and placed between the existing trees rather than cutting all of the trees out to build an inexpensive massive parking lot.

84

5.29

5.30

5.31

5.32 Plantings along a central walk on the University of California Los Angeles (UCLA) campus almost completely hide the adjacent campus classroom buildings and provide a garden-like environment.

5.33 Repetition of raised planting areas, trees and an interesting paving pattern on the UCLA campus.

5.34 A study, eating and sitting area on the edge of the major building on the UCLA campus.

5.34

86

5.35 *A sitting area off the main traffic route on the UCLA campus. Extensive plantings provide a quiet and serene atmosphere.*

5.36 Dry-style landscape used on the headquarters building of Sentry Insurance in Scottsdale, Arizona.

Corporate Headquarters. A trend among corporations in many areas of the country is to relocate their business offices in spacious suburban areas, away from crowded urban centers. In doing so, most of these clients have selected sites that provide opportunities for extensive landscaping. Water can be used to an extent that it may not be possible in other projects, and bodies of water or small streams may be natural parts of the site, which the designer would want to develop for aesthetic value. Outdoor areas for sitting and eating lunch should be a fundamental part of the planning, but depending on the needs of the client, a project might also contain elaborate recreation facilities, even swimming pools. The additional development and maintenance expenses at such sites have been justified by improved employee morale and public recognition of a favorable corporate image. During the past two decades some of the most significant building and landscape designs have been initiated by corporate clients.

5.37 Plantings which focus on the employee's entrance to an IBM office building in Atlanta, Georgia.

5.38

5.39

5.40

5.38 A small shopping center near Atlanta, Georgia, which used extensive plantings around its periphery.

5.39 Extensive plantings in this parking lot at a shopping center near Atlanta, Georgia, provide an attractive atmosphere and reduce the bleakness normally associated with parking lots.

5.40 An area which serves as a retention basin for storm water from the parking lots of the adjacent shopping center shown in the background. The area is made attractive by expansive plantings.

Shopping Centers. The design of malls in shopping centers allows a designer to use more variety than he can in other projects of similar size and scale. Indeed, the more variety the better, for if a shopper feels encouraged to stop, or change his direction, or rest for a while, he will presumable stay in the shopping center longer, think of additional things to buy, and see shops he never noticed before. To help achieve these things, the designer tries to create the widest possible variety of experience, not only with plants, but also with paving patterns, the creation of small resting places and alcoves, mounds, raised planters, fountains, seating, and other things.

Since most shopping centers provide some protection from wind and frost, more exotic species can be used in the planting areas. Most trees selected are specimens and each can act as a focal point in a small space. In larger, open areas, informal masses of small trees or shrubs might be used. In general, shrubs should also be flowering, though some evergreens are important for winter color. Those shrubs that are brightly colored and fragrant are especially useful. Many successfully planted shopping center malls contain beds of flowers in which spring bulbs, summer annuals, and autumn chrysanthemums are rotated.

The cost of maintenance of flower beds is high, but many shopping center developers advertise the beauty of a well planted mall and use seasonal flower displays as an attraction for potential shoppers, who more often than compensate them for the increased cost.

In recent years many new malls have been enclosed for year-round climate control and increased customer comfort. Less space is usually devoted to plants in contrast to the older style unenclosed mall. Some enclosed malls provide light wells where the limited interior plantings can prosper while others rotate plants to a green house to keep them healthy. On such malls exterior plantings emphasize entrances, screen parking lots and service areas and soften large expanses of bare building walls.

5.41 *Two Flowering Dogwood (Cornus florida) at Westchester Reform Temple, Scarsdale, New York.*

A. E. Bye and Associates

5.42   A. E. Bye and Associates

5.43

5.42 *Entrance planting at Westchester Reform Temple. Two Cutleaf Weeping Birch underplanted with Spreading English Yew. Note the contrasts of horizontals against verticals, dark forms against white, evergreens against deciduous.*

5.43 *Flush headstones are characteristic in the Punch Bowl National Cemetery in Honolulu, Hawaii.*

Church Landscapes. As suburbs have developed the construction of new church buildings has followed. In general larger sites are available and more attention can be paid to landscape development than when churches were located on small downtown sites. Parking is a prime consideration for suburban sites as the car must be accommodated. Parking does not have to be unsightly as islands for trees and screen shrubs can be developed to relieve the asphalt desert which parking lots often become.

Depending upon the needs of a particular denomination, outdoor courtyards and settings for garden weddings can be part of the site design. There may be a need for a worship garden which may be a focal point for a religious sculpture or symbol. Planting design needs to reflect the requirements for quietness, subdued activity, and protection from wind that are part of the liturgical functions of a particular church.

Social functions typically are separate from liturgical ones, and the design of these areas may be quite different to reflect the differences in function. Some churches will even set aside space for softball, volleyball, etc., as well as picnic areas. Playgrounds may be designed as part of a church school program. Where children are a planned part of the church program, one denomination has directed landscape architects to refrain from using plants which bear fruits and nuts near entrances or walks where children can pick them and drop them on carpets or throw them at other children. Also, large trees are not to be planted close to the building which would facilitate youth climbing on the roof of the church.

Cemeteries. There has been a transition during the past few decades from a complex and ornate expression of cemetery design to a simple one. Whereas cemeteries used to feature massings of shrubs and flowers in addition to tree plantings, around large headstones, today shrub plantings are kept to a minimum, headstones are kept flat, and the total area is given a sense of openness.

The main cause of this change is the cost of maintenance. Upright headstones and masses of shrubs and flowers are expensive to maintain, and a poorly maintained cemetery full of weeds and unmown grass is depressing. Lower cost can be realized by reducing shrub planting to a few locations at entrances and around buildings, by keeping trees few in number, and by developing large, open lawn spaces in which headstones are flush with the ground. Such a cemetery will be pleasant aesthetically. Best aesthetic quality is obtained when tree plantings are informal.

Avoid straight rows or the excessive repetition of one species. A few trees with flower color will add the attraction of color, and those blooming near the end of May will be especially pleasant.

The few shrub masses that may be necessary should generally have a strong horizontal form to fit the scale of a cemetery, though the precise character of the design will be dictated by any structural facilities at the site.

Land Reclamation. In recent decades surface mining of coal, minerals and gravel has dramatically increased. In most instances it has adversely affected the landscape. Laws have been passed which have regulated such activity and required the restoration or rehabilitation of the landscape. Landscape Architects and many other consultants have been involved in this process. The loss of topsoil and the exposure of toxic substances to the surface from sub-soils are just a few of the many problems facing rehabilitation.

Re-establishing vegetation becomes important to stabilize soil to prevent surface erosion, provide habitat for wildlife, future trees for wood, and grass for grazing and animal production.

Plants which are readily adaptable for the particular environmental conditions present should be used. Where adequate rainfall is present the re-establishment of plant growth is more rapidly facilitated, but in arid areas the recovery period is very slow.

The extraction of gravel close to existing residential areas requires additional considerations. These include noise and dust control as well as screening for aesthetic purposes. The creation of berms with the planting of a variety of evergreen and deciduous trees before the project begins help alleviate objections to the gravel extraction. If rehabilitation of the site is planned ahead and carried out during the extraction process, the site can be ready for other uses when the extraction is completed. In areas close to cities, parks and recreation areas can be one such use. Where water tables are high, a pond or lake can result after the extraction process has been completed. By arranging the overburden in a preplanned way gravel companies may obtain som economic advantage from the future sale of such areas which could include home sites adjacent to the water and recreation facilities such as boating, water skiing, swimming, and fishing.

Rights of Ways. Besides highways and streets we will also consider power lines and pipe lines. All of them have had considerable impact upon the landscape in recent years. Where careful planning has been done, their institution has been less noticeable than otherwise. power and pipe lines can be planned and routed so that the disruption to the existing landscape is minimal. They can be routed such that they can hardly be seen and the existing aesthetics maintained. Power poles and structures can be painted to blend into the existing landscape rather than contrasting with it which creates visual blight or pollution.

Highway routes can be located to blend into the existing landscape as well. Cut and fill can be reduced and gentle movement of the alignment reduces driver fatigue. Minimizing the scars to the existing landscape makes it easier to repair the damage and get new vegetation established. In arid areas the use of native plants is adviseable to save precious water resources though some initial irrigation to get the plants established is necessary, and supplemental water during dry periods keep the plants healthier.

In general new plantings for highways need to provide sufficient variety to relieve monotony yet not so much variety especially close to the driving lanes that the driver becomes tense. Informal groupings to trees

5.44 This view illustrates the vegetation pattern in a forest before a right-of-way is cleared. Typical right-of-way clearance is illustrated in the middle view. The transition from low to tall vegetation shown at the bottom is a better solution to right-of-way management.

5.45 This structure, containing microwave equipment of the Mountain Bell System at Vail, Colorado, was carefully designed to complement the landscape. It blends with the massive mountain scenery of the area better than exposed steel cross members would.

along the edge of the right-of-way seems preferred to straight rows of evenly spaced trees. In situations were roads are routed through existing forests, selective cutting of trees to form an irregular edge along the highway creates interest and reduces monotony. If views are available, occasional clear-cutting to open up and enframe such views adds considerable to the aesthetics of a highway. Locating rest stops in existing tree groupings provides immediate shade, is aesthetic and aids the driver.

Selective Designing: Natural Landscapes. Sometimes the development of a planting design does not require preparing a planting plan and specifying new plants to be installed. Some large parks in wilderness areas of the country have plenty of existing vegetation. When a wilderness area is opened for public use, the need may not be for more planting but for the development of views from highways, visitor centers, and campgrounds. The design of such aesthetic effects can be accomplished by selective thinning or removal of plants. Low branches on trees can be pruned to provide a view between the trunks of large trees to a lake or a distant mountain peak. Where necessary, some trees and under planting may be removed to reveal the vista, but care should be taken to retain some of the existing material to frame the view.

In their quest for neatness, many property owners who landscape new houses built in natural areas completely eliminate the undergrowth in favor of growing lawns. Grass cannot usually survive in the light that reaches the ground in wooded areas; the lawn fails, leaving the property owner frustrated. Many wooded natural areas, if left undisturbed, will

5.46   USDA Forest Service

5.46 A pipeline laid with minimum damage to the natural landscape. The pipe was pulled into place by cable, thus preventing damage to the site by trucks and other heavy equipment. The sod was carefully removed and stored.

5.47 The trench shown in 5.46 was filled and the sod was replaced after the pipe was laid. Very little change in the landscape is visible.

5.47   USDA Forest Service

96

California State Department of Transportation

5.48 *Rest areas along limited access highways provide several useful functions besides relief from the monotony of high-speed travel. When thoughtfully designed they provide an optimum of function and comfort. This rest area is near Artois, California.*

maintain themselves. All such a "landscape design" requires is a willingness by the client to tolerate less neatness in the landscape and to derive increased enjoyment from the diversity nature offers with wildflowers and other forms of undergrowth, and with wildlife.

SUMMARY

Through his training in design, botany, horticulture, and ecology, coupled with some practical experience, the designer prepares himself to resolve complex planting design problems. There are many aspects of his work that pose problems he may not be able to resolve himself; for resolution of these he will need the services of others whose training and expertise will bring together the information and resources necessary for satisfactory, functional, and aesthetically pleasing landscapes.

5.49

5.50

5.49, 5.50 *A forested slope shown both before and after timber was harvested with careful attention to the aesthetic appearance of the slope.*

Appendix 5-A
Selecting Plants with a Computer

The use of a computer can speed up and expand a designer's use of plants. There is a commercially available software program called CAPS (computer-augmented plant selection) which is easy to learn and easy to use. It is available for several brands of microcomputers. For more information contact PDA Publishers, 1725 East Fountain, Mesa, Arizona, 85203, or Susan Schmieman at Terisan, P. O. Box 1442, Silver Spring, Maryland, 20902.

Furnished with this software are several plant data bases. These include a file on trees, one for shrubs, and one for ground covers and vines. Additional data bases are planned for regional plants, herbaceous plants, etc. The user can add plants until a file reaches 300, but new files can be created which means there is no upper limit to the number of plants that can be accessed by the software. Many designer-users may want to create separate plant files for the native plants used in their own geographical area. More than one floppy disk may be required to handle all of the data bases that a designer may want to use. Using a hard disk would simplify and speed up the process of adding to and searching the data bases.

Illustrated at the end of this appendix is the criteria used to describe each plant when it is entered into the data base and also to search for plants during the design phase. There are 210 potential individual characteristics comprising a total of 26 different categories. These can be modified to fit your particular needs, such as expanding the USDA hardiness zones for warmer climates.

Up to 25 criteria can be used at one time by the computer to search each data base file for plants you may want to use in a particular design situation. The larger the number of criteria, the fewer the list of plants that will be selected. It is possible with large numbers that the computer will not find a plant that fits or meets all the criteria specified.

CAPS plant criteria

1. *HARDINESS ZONE (USDA)
2. zone 2 (-50 to -40 degrees F.)
3. zone 3 (-40 to -30 degrees F.)
4. zone 4 (-30 to -20 degrees F.)
5. zone 5 (-20 to -10 degrees F.)
6. zone 6 (-10 to 0 degrees F.)

7. *SITE SOIL TYPE
8. clay--->clay loam
9. silt--->silt loam
10. sand--->sandy loam
11. gravel--->gravelly loam

12. *SITE DRAINAGE
13. dry soils
14. wet soils
15. moist soils
16. moist/well-drained soils

17. *SOIL FERTILITY
18. average fertility
19. low fertility

20. *SOIL pH
21. <5.5, strongly acid soil
22. 5.5-6.5, moderate-slight acid
23. 6.5-7.5, neutral soil
24. 7.5-8.5, slight-moderate basic
25. >8.5, strongly basic soil

26. *LIGHT CONDITIONS
27. full sun, direct, all day
28. half shade, 1/2 day full sun
29. light shade, filtered sunlight
30. open shade, north of bldg.
31. full shade, dense cover
32. other light conditions

33. *ENVIRONMENTAL TOLERANCES
34. tolerates poor drainage
35. tolerates drought conditions
36. tolerates road salt
37. tolerates air pollution
38. tolerates urban conditions
39. other tolerances

40. *PLANT TYPE
41. deciduous
42. evergreen
43. semi-evergreen
44. broadleaf evergreen

45. *PLANT FORM/HABIT
46. rounded form
47. oval form
48. vase-shape
49. pyramidal form
50. columnar form
51. irregular form/habit
52. arching habit
53. upright habit
54. spreading habit
55. horizontal habit
56. pendulous habit
57. prostrate habit
58. low branching habit
59. other form/habit

60. *MATURE HEIGHT
61. <1' height
62. 1-3' height
63. 3-8' height
64. 8-15' height
65. 15-25' height
66. 25-40' height
67. 40-60' height
68. >60' height

69. *MATURE SPREAD
70. <1' spread
71. 1-3' spread
72. 3-6' spread
73. 6-10' spread
74. 10-15' spread
75. 15-25' spread
76. 25-40' spread
77. 40-60' spread
78. >60' spread

79. *ROOT SYSTEMS
80. fibrous roots
81. tap root
82. fleshy root
83. shallow roots
84. deep roots
85. easily transplanted
86. spring transplant preferred
87. roots fix nitrogen
88. difficult to transplant
89. transplant B&B
90. other root characteristics

91. *PLANT DENSITY
92. heavy density
93. average density
94. open density

95. *NOTABLE TRUNK/STEM FEATURES
96. spines/thorns
97. tendrils
98. multi-trunked
99. climbing/twining vine
100. colorful twigs/branches
101. other trunk/stem features

102. *LEAF SIZE/TEXTURE
103. <1" leaf/extra fine
104. 1-3" leaf/fine
105. 3-6" leaf/medium
106. 6-12" leaf/coarse
107. >12" leaf/extra coarse
108. leaflets
109. needle-like leaf
110. scale-like leaf
111. other leaf character

112. *FRUIT
113. insignificant fruit
114. ornamental fruit value
115. white fruit
116. cream fruit
117. light pink fruit
118. deep pink fruit
119. red fruit
120. red orange fruit
121. orange fruit
122. yellow orange fruit
123. yellow fruit
124. green fruit
125. blue fruit
126. purple fruit
127. black fruit
128. brown fruit
129. other fruit color

130. *FLOWER COLOR/PERIOD
131. insignificant flower
132. late winter bloom (Feb-Mar)
133. early spring bloom (Mar-Apr)
134. mid spring bloom (Apr-May)
135. late spring bloom (May-June)
136. early summer bloom (June-July)
137. mid summer bloom (July-Aug)
138. late summer bloom (Aug-Sept)
139. early fall bloom (Sept-Oct)
140. mid fall bloom (Oct-Nov)
141. white bloom
142. cream bloom
143. light pink bloom
144. deep pink bloom
145. red bloom
146. red orange bloom
147. orange bloom
148. yellow orange bloom
149. yellow bloom
150. yellow green bloom
151. green bloom
152. blue green bloom
153. blue bloom
154. violet bloom
155. fragrant plant parts
156. other flower characteristic

157. *SUMMER LEAF COLOR
158. light green (yellow- or gray-)
159. med. green summer color
160. dark green summer color
161. blue green summer color
162. bronze (reddish/greenish) s.l.c
163. glossy leaves
164. other summer leaf character

165. *FALL LEAF COLOR
166. early fall color/Sept
167. mid fall color/Oct
168. late fall color/Nov
169. muted yellow fall color
170. yellow green fall color
171. bright yellow fall color
172. muted red fall color
173. bright red fall color
174. muted orange fall color
175. bright orange fall color
176. light brown fall color
177. dark brown fall color
178. green fall color/inc.evergrns
179. bronze fall color
180. other fall color

181. *SIGNIFICANT BARK CHARACTER
182. coarse bark
183. smooth bark
184. smooth bark w/lenticels
185. exfoliating bark
186. very dark bark
187. very light bark
188. reddish bark
189. other bark character

190. *STRONG VISUAL FEATURES
191. notable fall foliage
192. notable spring flowers
193. notable summer flowers
194. notable fall flowers
195. notable spring fruit
196. notable summer fruit
197. notable fall fruit
198. notable winter fruit
199. notable plant form
200. attractive bark
201. other notable features

202. *LEAF DROP DATE
203. late summer/early fall leaf dr.
204. mid fall leaf drop
205. late fall/early winter leaf dr.

206. *GROWTH RATE
207. slow growth
208. moderate growth
209. rapid growth

210. *PLANT PROBLEMS
211. no problems
212. occasional pests/disease
213. troublesome pests/disease
214. slow to establish
215. messy fruit
216. invasive root system
217. weak-wooded
218. poisonous plant parts
219. bad odor
220. needs sun/wind protection
221. short lived
222. difficult to obtain
223. other plant problems

224. *FUNCTIONAL USES
225. erosion control
226. windbreaks
227. wildlife food/habitat
228. naturalizing
229. low maintenance
230. hedge planting
231. screen planting
232. specimen planting
233. street planting
234. border or mass planting

235. *USER DEFINED CATEGORY
236. user defined
237. user defined
238. user defined
239. user defined

240. **End of File**

GENERAL UNITED STATES

Dirr, Michael A., 1983. *Manual of Woody Landscape Plants*, Third Edition. Champaign, Illinois: Stipes Publishing, 826 pages.

Flint, Harrison L., 1983. *Landscape Plants for Eastern North America*. New York: John Wiley, 677 pages.

Hillier Color Dictionary of Trees & Shrubs. 1982. New York: Van Nostrand Reinhold, 323 pages.

Johnson, Hugh, 1973. *International Book of Trees*. London: Mirchell Beazley Publishers Ltd., 288 pages.

Johnson, H. & Miles, P., 1981. *Pocket Guide to Garden Plants*. New York: Simon & Schuster, 192 pages.

Wyman, Donald, 1971. *Trees for American Gardens*. New York: MacMillan, 502 pages.

Wyman, Donald, 1971. *Shrubs and Vines for American Gardens*. New York: MacMillan, 613 pages.

ARIZONA AND CALIFORNIA

Duffield, M.R. & Jones, W.D., 1981. *Plants for Dry Climates*. Tucson, Arizona: H.P. Books, 176 pages.

Perry, Robert C., 1981. *Trees and Shrubs for Dry California Landscapes*. San Dimas, California: Land Design Publishing, 184 pages.

Sunset Books, 1979. *New Western Garden Book*. Menlo Park, California: Lane Publishing, 512 pages.

Sutliff, Dale A., 1983. *How to Choose a Plant When You Need One: A Guide for Plant Selection*. San Luis Obispo, California: (published by the author), 102 pages.

(also, see books listed in General United States)

PACIFIC NORTHWEST

McClintock, E. & Leiser, A. *An Annotated Checklist of Wood Ornamental Plants of California, Oregon and Washington*. Berkeley, California: Agricultural Sciences Publications, University of California, 134 pages.

(also, see books listed in General United States)

SOUTHEASTERN UNITED STATES

Duncan, W.H. & Foote, L.E., 1975. *Wildflowers of the Southeastern United States*. Athens, Georgia: University of Georgia Press.

Halfacre, R.G. & Shawcroft, A.R., 1979. *Landscape Plants of the Southeast*. Raleigh, North Carolina: Sparks Press.

Harrer, E.S. & J.G., 1962. *Guide to Southern Trees*. Second Edition. New York: Dover.

Martin, E.C. Jr., 1983. *Landscape Plants in Design*. Westport, Connecticut: AVI Publishing Co., 497 pages.

Odenwald, N.G. & Turner, J.R., 1980. *Plants for the South*. Baton Rouge, Louisiana: Claitor Law Publishing, 585 pages.

Radford, A.E., Ahles, H.E. & Bell, C.R., 1968. *Manual of the Vascular Flora of the Carolinas*. Chapel Hill, North Carolina: University of North Carolina Press.

Watkins, John V., 1975. *Florida Landscape Plants*. Gainesville, Florida: University of Florida Press, 420 pages.

Whitcomb, C.E., 1975. *Know It and Grow It*. Tulsa, Oklahoma: Oil Capital Printing Co., 500 pages.

Wigginton, B.E., 1963. *Trees and Shrubs for the Southeast*. Athens, Georgia: University of Georgia Press.

Workman, Richard, 1980. *Growing Native*. Sanibel, Florida: Sanibel-Captiva Conservation Fund, 136 pages.

(also, see references listed under General United States)

Appendix 5-C
State Nursery Associations

Alabama

Alabama Nurserymen's Association
860 Terrace Acres
Auburn, AL 36830

Arizona

Arizona Nurserymen's Association
444 West Camelback Road, Suite 302
Phoenix, AZ 85013

Arkansas

Arkansas Nurserymen's Association
P.O. Box 5495
North Little Rock, AR 72119

California

California Association of
   Nurserymen
1419 21st Street
Sacramento, CA 95814

Colorado

Colorado Nurserymen's Association
10775 North 65th Street
Longmont, CO 80501

Connecticut

Connecticut Nurserymen's
   Association
30 Lafayette Square #109
Vernon, CT 06066

Delaware

Delaware Association of
   Nurserymen
RFD #3, Box 56
Harrington, DE 19952

Florida

Florida Foliage Association
P.O. Box Y
Apopka, FL 32703

Florida Nurserymen's & Growers
   Association
5401 Kirkman Rd. #650
Orlando, FL 32819

Georgia

Georgia Nurserymen's Association
190 Springtree Rd.
Athens, GA 30605

Hawaii

Hawaii Association of Nurserymen
P.O. Box 293
Honolulu, HI 96809

Idaho

Idaho Nursery Association
1615 N. Woodruff
Idaho Falls, ID 83401

Illinois

Illinois State Nurserymen's
   Association
Springfield Hilton #1702
Springfield, IL 62701

Indiana

Indiana Association of Nurserymen
Entomology Hall
Purdue University
West Lafayette, IN 47907

Iowa

Iowa Nurserymen's Association
7261 NW 21st Street
Ankeny, IA 50021

Kansas

Kansas Nurserymen's Association
Blueville Nursery, Route 1
Manhattan, KS 66502

Kentucky

Kentucky Nurserymen's Association
701 Baxter Ave.
Louisville, KY 40204

Louisiana

Louisiana Association of
   Nurserymen
P.O. Box 4492
University of Southwestern Louisiana
Lafayette, LA 70501

Maine

Maine Nurserymen's Association
Plant & Soil Department
SMVTI, Fort Road
South Portland, ME 04106

Maryland

Maryland Nurserymen's Association
2800 Elnora St.
Silver Spring, MD 20902

Massachusetts

Massachusetts Nurserymen's
    Association
715 Boylston Street
Boston, MA 02116

Michigan

Michigan Association of Nurserymen
5127 Aurelius Rd.
Lansing, MI 48910

Minnesota

Minnesota Nurserymen's Association
P.O. Box 13307
St. Paul, MN 55113

Mississippi

Mississippi Nurserymen's Association
P.O. Box 5207
Mississippi, MS 39762

Missouri

Missouri Association of Nurserymen
Raytown Nursery
7911 Spring Valley Road
Raytown, MO 64138

Montana

Montana Association of Nurserymen
P.O. Box 1871
Bozeman, MT 59715

Nebraska

Nebraska Nurserymen's Association
P.O. Box 6306
Lincoln, NE 68506

Nevada

Nevada Nurserymen's Association
651 Avenue B
Boulder City, NV 89005

New Hampshire

New Hampshire Plant Growers
    Association
194 Rumford Street
Concord, NH 03440

New Jersey

New Jersy Association of
    Nurserymen
c/o Lawrence D. Little, Jr.
Box 231 Cook College
New Brunswick, NJ 08903

New Mexico

New Mexico Association of
    Nurserymen
P.O. Box 1803
Corrales, NM 87048

New York

New York Nurserymen's Association
310 Madison Ave.
New Nork, NY 10017

North Carolina

North Carolina Nurserymen's
    Association
Wilder's Nursery, Route 2
Knightdale, NC 27545

North Dakota

North Dakota Nursery & Greenhouse
    Association
P.O. Box 5658
Pargo, ND 58105

Ohio

Ohio Nurserymen's Association
2021 E. Dublin-Granville Rd. #185
Columbus, OH 43229

Oklahoma

Oklahoma Nurserymen's Association
400 N. Portland
Oklahoma, City, OK 73107

Oregon

Oregon Association of Nurserymen
2780 S.E. Harrison
Suite 204
Portland, OR 97222

Pennsylvania

Pennsylvania Nurserymen's Association
234 State Street
Harrisburg, PA 17101

Rhode Island

Rhode Island Nurserymen's
    Association
c/o J.J. McGuire
University of Rhode Island
Kingston, RI 02881

South Carolina

South Carolina Nurserymen's
    Association
Department of Horticulture
Clemson University
Clemson, SC 29631

South Dakota

South Dakota Nurserymen's
    Association
Johnson Nursery & Garden Center
3401 E. 10th Street
Sioux Falls, SD 57103

Tennessee

Tennessee Nurserymen's Association
P.O. Box 57
McMinnville, TN 37110

Texas

Texas Association of Nurserymen
512 East Riverside Drive, Suite 207
Austin, TX 78704

Utah

Utah Association of Nurserymen
3500 South 9th East
Salt Lake City, UT 84106

Vermont

Vermont Plantsman's Association
c/o Robert K. Chipman
Bradford, VT 05033

Virginia

Virginia Nurserymen's Association
P.O. Box 827
Richmond, VA 23207

Washington

Washington State Nurserymen's
    Association
P.O. Box 670
Sumner, WA 98390

West Virginia

West Virginia Nurserymen's
    Association
Route 2, Box 89
Beckley, WV 25801

Wisconsin

Wisconsin Nurserymen's Association
Route 1, Box 377
Lake Mills, WI 53551

CANADA –

Atlantic Provinces

Atlantic Provinces Nursery
    Trades Association
209 Shore Drive
Bedford, NS B4A 2E7 Canada

Alberta

Landscape Alberta Nursery
    Trades Association
10215 176th Street
Edmonton, Alberta T5S 1M1 Canada

British Columbia

B.C. Nursery Trades Association
10330 152nd Street, Suite 230
Surrey, BC V3R 4G8 Canada

Manitoba

Manitoba Nursery Trades Association
104 Parkside Drive
Winnipeg, Manitoba R3J 3P8 Canada

Ontario

Landscape Ontario Horticultural
    Trades Association
3034 Palstan Road, Suite 103
Missisauga, Ontario L4Y 2Z6 Canada

Quebec

Association Paysage Quebec
Jardines Van Den Hende
University Lavel
Ste. Foy, Quebec G1K 7P4 Canada

Saskatchewan

Saskatchewan Nursery Trades
    Association
Box 460
Carnduff, Sask S0C 0S0 Canada

6

Preparing Planting Plans

PLANS

The development of drafting skills and an understanding of the common graphic symbolism used for plans is a prerequisite to the preparation of planting plans. The elementary aspects of drafting will not be discussed here, because the skills are best acquired in a course where an instructor demonstrates them, monitors student progress frequently, and corrects errors and weaknesses quickly.

Professional designers prepare themselves through a number of college courses over a period of time generally exceeding three years. During that time, drafting and graphic skills are usually acquired in combination with background in a variety of problems in design, planting design, and construction. The designer's skills mature through internship, following graduation, for a period averaging from three to five years under the guidance of an experienced landscape architect or designer. The quality of workmanship on the drawings is as important as the quality of the design. Well-prepared, neat drawings make a positive impression upon both the client and the contractor.

Most states now require the registration or licensing of those who wish to call themselves landscape architects or practice landscape architecture (this varies from state to state), which mean their plans and specifications must be stamped or bear a seal showing evidence of their compliance with the law. A number of states allow nurserymen and others who call themselves "landscape designers" to prepare the planting plans. The preparation of planting plans for government projects in many states can be accomplished only by licensed (or registered) landscape architects.

Plans at best are very poor representations of the final completed project. They represent a view looking straight down from overhead, a view rarely if ever seen by the client. Most clients have difficulty understanding what they read on the plan or comprehending how the finished project will look on the basis of the drawing, but if the client is confident about the designer and trusts him, he need not feel insecure if he does not know what the graphic symbols mean. A good client will respect the abilities and reputation of his designer and will rely on his judgment and recommendations. The principal purpose of a plan is to convey the intent of the designer to the contractor, and drawings currently provide the best known means of serving this purpose.

The plans or drawings, combined with any drawings of planting details such as those illustrated in this chapter, along with the specifications, are a part of the contract document used for a project. The preparation of specifications is discussed later in Chapter 7, and the specifications written for an actual project are reprinted in an appendix at the end of that chapter.

In projects where clients need a fuller visualization of the final appearance of a project than they see with the aerial plans, perspective sketches or renderings are useful.

On the working drawings made as part of the planting plans, the exact location of each plant is shown. If there is room, the name of the plant should be written out; often an abbreviation is all there is room for. A designer should always work with the botanical name of a plant, providing a plant list, along with or as part of his drawings, on which are given the common name following the botanical name, total quantity, sizes, and other requirements for the plants.

Different symbols are used to illustrate a variety of plants. The scale of these drawings varies from project to project. It is difficult to show shrubs at a scale greater than 1 inch = 20 feet and the best scales are ⅛ inch = 1 foot or 1 inch = 10 feet. For showing the details of planting of perennials, annuals, etc., the best scale is ¼ inch = 1 foot.

It is rare that dimensions are placed on planting plans unless the location of a plant is quite critical. The contractor can usually place a scale or a measuring tape on the plan and determine the location of each plant with the accuracy needed.

When planting plans are prepared without specifications, a number of explanatory notes may be needed, otherwise these should be included in the specifications.

In a set of drawings one or more sheets following the planting plans will show various details. Some of these may include cross-sections through tree pits, staking arrangements, wells to protect existing trees when fill is added, and retaining walls to protect existing trees when the soil is cut below existing grades. In urban projects, trees may be planted in paved areas and raised planters. Both plan views and cross-sections may be needed to show the details necessary for the contractor.

All drawings should be prepared on material such as vellum, linen, or mylar, which will remain tough even after a drawing has been handled for a time, and from which photocopies of the drawings can be made. The original drawings will always remain the property of the designer. It is possible to photocopy a second reproducible tracing on either sepia-paper or mylar, and this may be given to the client for his own use. Contractors sometimes also use such tracings for preparing "as-built" drawings which they return to the landscape architect following completion of the project.

Black-line or blue-line ozalid or diazo reproductions are generally made from the original drawings and are prepared in sets issued to contractors invited to bid on the project. After bid opening the sets of drawings are reclaimed by the landscape architect and reissued to the successful bidder for his use during construction.

COST ESTIMATING

Most planting design projects will require that a cost estimate be prepared. Many clients will establish a budget for the designer, and a cost estimate will assist in determining how well a design fits the budget. A computer can be a valuable tool in preparing a cost estimate as it does all the computing, and revisions are very simple and quick to make an important consideration when a project goes over budget, revisions must be made, and a deadline is hours away.

Several commercial software programs are available which can be used. Or, you can design one yourself with a relational database management system such as Condor 3. The illustrations accompanying this section were prepared by the author using the Condor rDBMS software which is available for many brands of microcomputers. A few hours of study in the software manual were required to become familiar with the commands and walk through the design, formatting and entering of data into the data base. Printouts (also called hard copy) are facilitated by the "report" command on this software. Revisions are accomplished by the "update" command which allows you to change one or any number of items in your estimate whether it is quantity, unit price, or just to correct a misspelled word. After the corrections the "report" command will quickly recompute the estimate and print a new hardcopy.

In the estimate illustrated, plants are grouped by size and an average price per group is used. Plants can also be listed individually if you so desire and want to spend the time to enter them all into the data base. The estimate can be simple or complex depending upon your needs.

For those searching for cost information outside their own area, or as a cross-check for their own cost-data files, it may be helpful to secure a copy of *Cost Data for Landscape Construction* available from Kerr Associates, 1942 Irving Avenue South, Minneapolis, Minnesota, 55403. This paperback book is updated and published annually.

The first illustration, which follows, shows the categories of information which are to be entered into the data base. These categories are on the left of the colon (:) and on the right is the items entered by the user once the data base is designed, formatted, defined and ready to accept data (a process that is easy to do by using the manual that is supplied with the software). You can see the sample item included in the second illustration – the final cost estimate as it was printed out by the "report" command.

```
JOB.NAME :LIBRARY PARK
SECT :Irrigation
ITEM :Pop-up Lawn Spray Head
QUAN :    386
TYPE :each
MAT.UNIT :   14.00
LAB.UNIT :    7.00


JOB.NAME :LIBRARY PARK
SECT :Irrigation
ITEM :Valves, boxes, wiring
QUAN :     15
TYPE :each
MAT.UNIT :  149.00
LAB.UNIT :   70.00


JOB.NAME :LIBRARY PARK
SECT :Planting
ITEM :Mulch and herbicide
QUAN :  5978
TYPE :sq.ft.
MAT.UNIT :     .20
LAB.UNIT :     .20


JOB.NAME :LIBRARY PARK
SECT :Planting
ITEM :Plants, 15 gal. size
QUAN :     63
TYPE :each
MAT.UNIT :   30.00
LAB.UNIT :   45.00


JOB.NAME :LIBRARY PARK
SECT :Prepare Site
ITEM :Top Soil
QUAN :    175
TYPE :cu.yd.
MAT.UNIT :   10.85
LAB.UNIT :     .00
```

WALKER-HARRIS-ASSOCIATES-INC.
1725 E. Fountain
Mesa Arizona 85203-5121
(602) 898-1624

****

02/13/85   Page 1

Cost Estimate for: LIBRARY PARK

Section: Irrigation

Item	Quan.	Unit Type	Material Unit Cost	Labor Unit Cost	Total Cost
Bubbler heads	381	each	$4.00	$2.00	$2286.00
Controller	1	each	1070.00	$285.00	$1355.00
Pop-up Lawn Spray Head	386	each	$14.00	$7.00	$8106.00
Pressure Vac. Breaker	1	each	$185.00	$95.00	$280.00
Valves, boxes, wiring	15	each	$149.00	$70.00	$3285.00

Section Total.. $15312.00

Section: Planting

Item	Quan.	Unit Type	Material Unit Cost	Labor Unit Cost	Total Cost
Mulch and herbicide	5978	sq.ft.	$.20	$.20	$2391.20
Lawn, hydro-seeded	26974	sq.ft.	$.02	$.04	$1618.44
Plants, 1 gal. size	79	each	$3.50	$7.00	$829.50
Plants, 15 gal. size	63	each	$30.00	$45.00	$4725.00
Plants, 5 gal. size	191	each	$7.50	$15.00	$4297.50

Section Total... $13861.64

Section: Prepare Site

Item	Quan.	Unit Type	Material Unit Cost	Labor Unit Cost	Total Cost
Top Soil	175	cu.yd.	$10.85	$.00	$1898.75
Fine Grading	2998	sq.yd.	$.00	$.78	$2338.44

Section Total... $4237.19

                              Total Cost Estimate $33410.83

Alternate Symbols for Plants

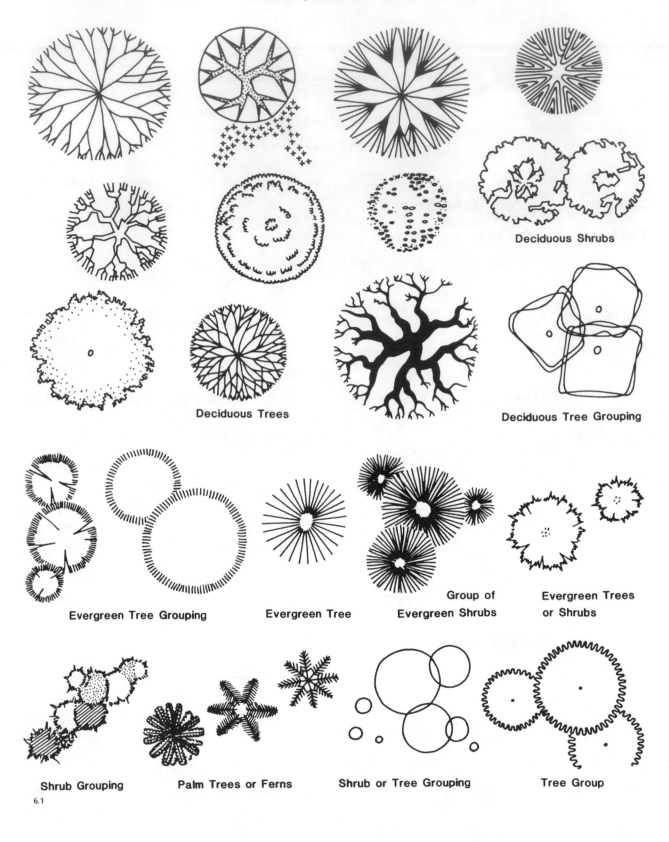

Deciduous Shrubs

Deciduous Trees

Deciduous Tree Grouping

Evergreen Tree Grouping   Evergreen Tree   Group of Evergreen Shrubs   Evergreen Trees or Shrubs

Shrub Grouping   Palm Trees or Ferns   Shrub or Tree Grouping   Tree Group

6.1

6.1 *These are some of the many alternative symbols that can be used to represent plants on plans.*

6.2 to 6.16 *This group of drawings illustrate the vast difference in graphic techniques and approaches that can be used by landscape architects to prepare planting plans.*

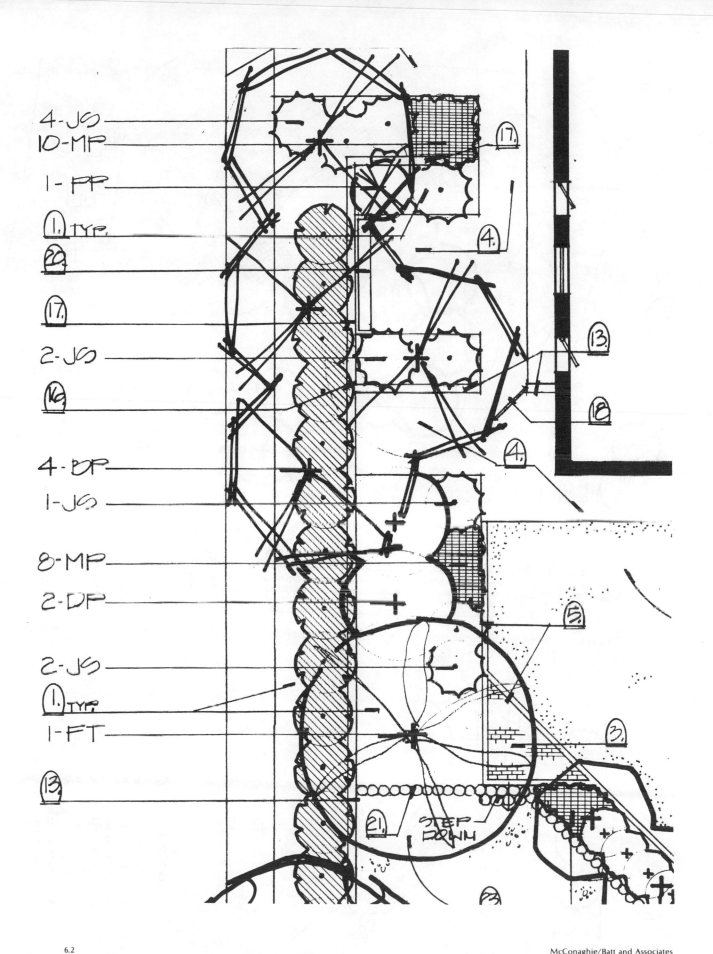

4-JS
10-MP

1-PP

1, TYP.

20

17.

2-JS

14

4-DP

1-JS

8-MP

2-DP

2-JS

1, TYP.

1-FT

13

17.

4.

13

18

4.

5.

3.

STEP DOWN

21.

23

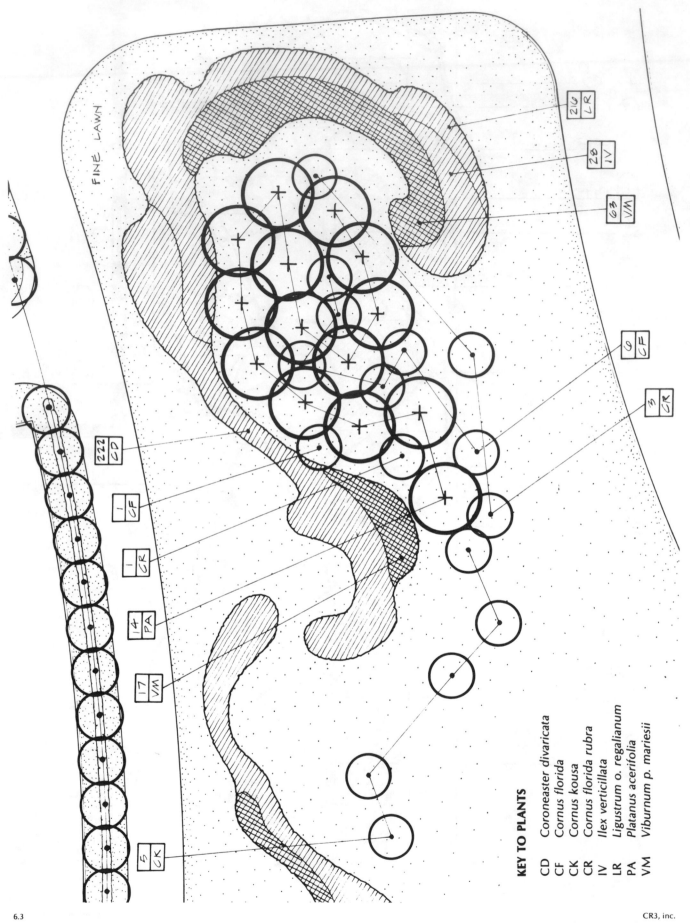

FINE LAWN

210 LR

20 IV

63 VM

0 CF

3 CR

222 CD

1 CF

1 CR

14 PA

17 VM

5 CK

KEY TO PLANTS

CD	*Coroneaster divaricata*
CF	*Cornus florida*
CK	*Cornus kousa*
CR	*Cornus florida rubra*
IV	*Ilex verticillata*
LR	*Ligustrum o. regalianum*
PA	*Platanus acerifolia*
VM	*Viburnum p. mariesii*

6.3

CR3, inc.

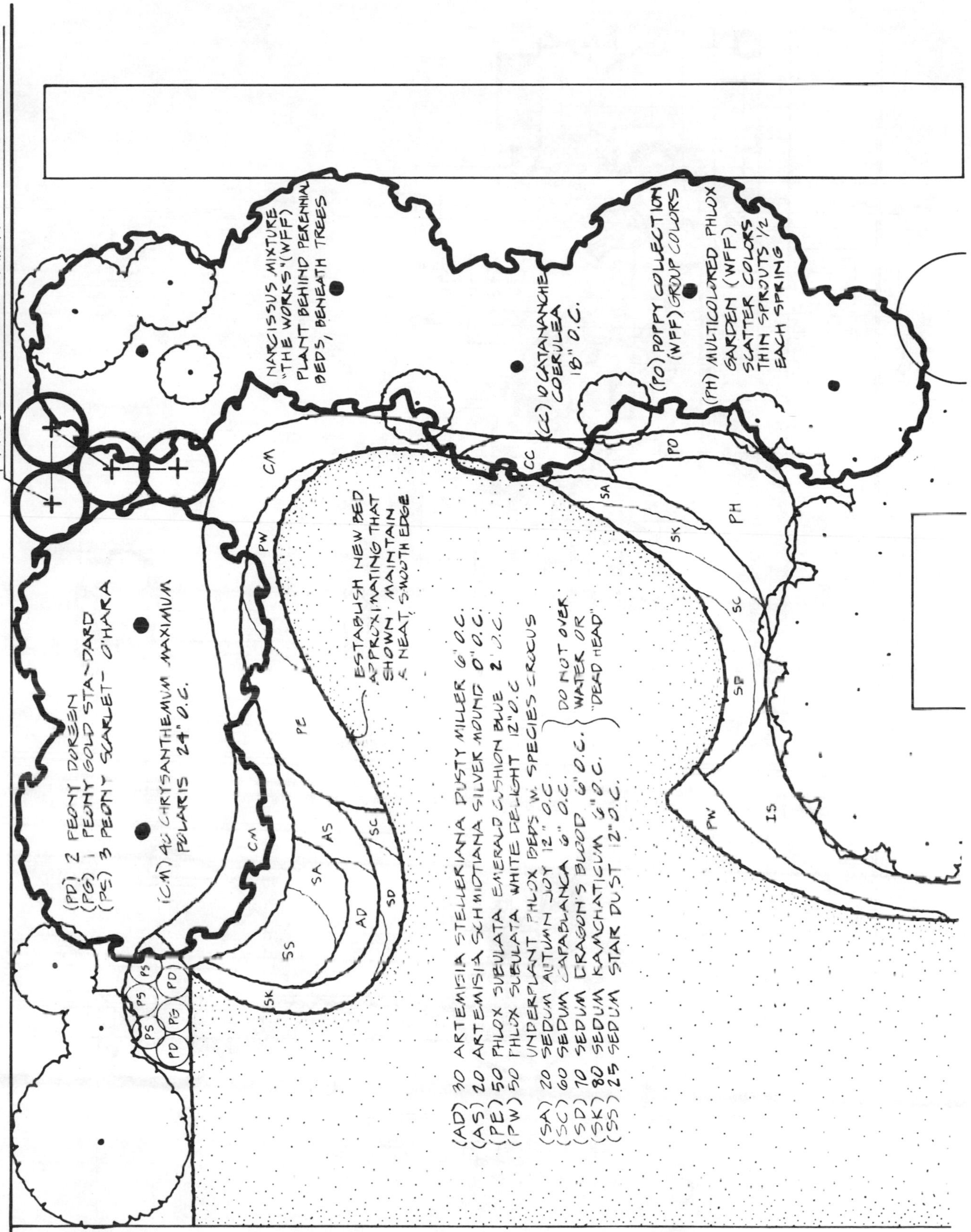

4 RHODODENDRON SMIRNOWII SCINTILLATION
(PD) 2 PEONY DOREEN
(PG) 1 PEONY GOLD STANDARD
(PS) 3 PEONY SCARLET O'HARA
(CM) 40 CHRYSANTHEMUM MAXIMUM POLARIS 24" O.C.
NARCISSUS MIXTURE "THE WORKS" (WFF) PLANT BEHIND PERENNIAL BEDS, BENEATH TREES
(CC) 10 CATANANCHE COERULEA 18" O.C.
(PO) POPPY COLLECTION (WFF) GROUP COLORS
(PH) MULTICOLORED PHLOX GARDEN (WFF) SCATTER COLORS THIN SPROUTS 1/2 EACH SPRING
ESTABLISH NEW BED APPROXIMATING THAT SHOWN. MAINTAIN A NEAT, SMOOTH EDGE
(AD) 30 ARTEMISIA STELLERIANA DUSTY MILLER 6" O.C.
(AS) 20 ARTEMISIA SCHMIDTIANA SILVER MOUND 0" O.C.
(PE) 50 PHLOX SUBULATA EMERALD CUSHION BLUE 2' O.C.
(PW) 50 PHLOX SUBULATA WHITE DELIGHT 12" O.C.
UNDERPLANT PHLOX BEDS W. SPECIES CROCUS
(SA) 20 SEDUM AUTUMN JOY 12" O.C.
(SC) 60 SEDUM CAPABLANCA 6" O.C.
(SD) 70 SEDUM DRAGON'S BLOOD 6" O.C.
(SK) 80 SEDUM KAMCHATICUM 6" O.C.
(SS) 25 SEDUM STAR DUST 12" O.C.
DO NOT OVER WATER OR "DEAD HEAD"
PD
PG
PS
CM
CC
PO
PH
SA
SK
SC
SP
PW
IS
PE
AS
SD
AD
SS

6.4

CR3, inc.

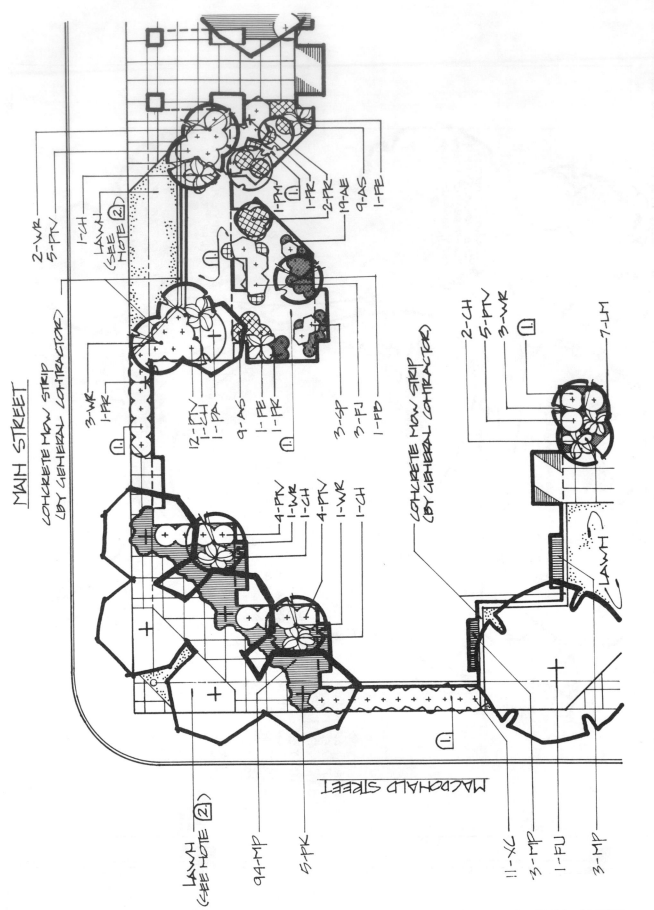

MAIN STREET

CONCRETE MOW STRIP
(BY GENERAL CONTRACTOR)

2-WR
5-PTV
1-CH
LAWN
(SEE NOTE ②)

1-PM
1-PR
2-PR
19-AE
9-AS
1-PE

3-WR
1-PR

12-PTV
1-CH
1-PA
9-AS
1-PE
1-PR

3-SP
3-FJ
1-PD

4-PTV
1-WR
1-CH
4-PTV
1-WR
1-CH

CONCRETE MOW STRIP
(BY GENERAL CONTRACTOR)

2-CH
5-PTV
3-WR
7-LM

LAWN

MACDONALD STREET

LAWN
(SEE NOTE ②)

94-MP

5-PK

11-XC
3-MP
1-FU
3-MP

Plant List

KEY	BOTANICAL NAME	COMMON NAME	QTY	SIZE
AE	*Apidistra elatior*	Cast-Iron Plant	19	10" pot
AS	*Asparagus sprengeri*	Sprenger Asparagus	20	5 gal.
CH	*Chamaerops humilis*	Mediterranean Fan Palm	16	24" box
EM	*Eucalyptus microtheca*	Coolibah Tree	40	24" box
FB	*Ficus benjamina*	Chinese Weeping Banyan	1	15 gal.
FE	*Ficus elastica 'decora'*	Broad-leaved Indian Rubber Plant	2	15 gal.
FJ	*Fatsia japonica*	Japanese Aralia	7	5 gal.
FR	*Ficus Repens*	Creeping Fig Vine	6	5 gal.
FU	*Fraxinus undei*	Shamel Ash	10	36" box
HC	*Hedera canariensis*	Algerian Ivy	44	1 gal.
JU	*Juniperus chinesis pfitzeriana 'compacta'*	Nick's Compact Pfitzer Juniper	37	5 gal.
LM	*Lantana montevidensis*	Trailing Lantana	33	5 gal.
MP	*Myoporum parvifolium*	Myoporum	412	1 gal.
NO	*Nerium oleander 'petite salmon'*	Dwarf Oleander	73	5 gal.
PA	*Prunus cerasifera 'krauter vesuvius'*	Krauter's Purple-leaf Plum	2	24" box
PE	*Pennisetum setaceum*	Fountain Grass	7	5 gal.
PK	*Pyrus kawakami*	Evergreen Pear	21	36" box
PM	*Podocarpus macrophyllus*	Yew Pine	1	24" box
PR	*Phoenix roebelenii*	Pigmy Date Palm	2	24" box
PS	*Philodendron selloum*	Selloum Philodendron	4	15 gal.
PTV	*Pittosporum tobira variegata*	Variegated Pittosporum	54	15 gal.
SP	*Spathiphyllum 'mauna loa'*	White Flag – Peace Lily	3	12" pot
SR	*Strelitzia reginae*	Tropical Bird of Paradise	3	5 gal.
XC	*Xylosma congestum*	Shiny Xylosma	62	5 gal.
XCE	*Xylosma congestum espalier*	Xylosma Espalier	4	15 gal.
WR	*Washintonia robusta*	Mexican Fan Palm	6	12' ht.

6.6

6.5 Planting plan for a bank.

6.6 Plant list for the planting plan in 6.5.

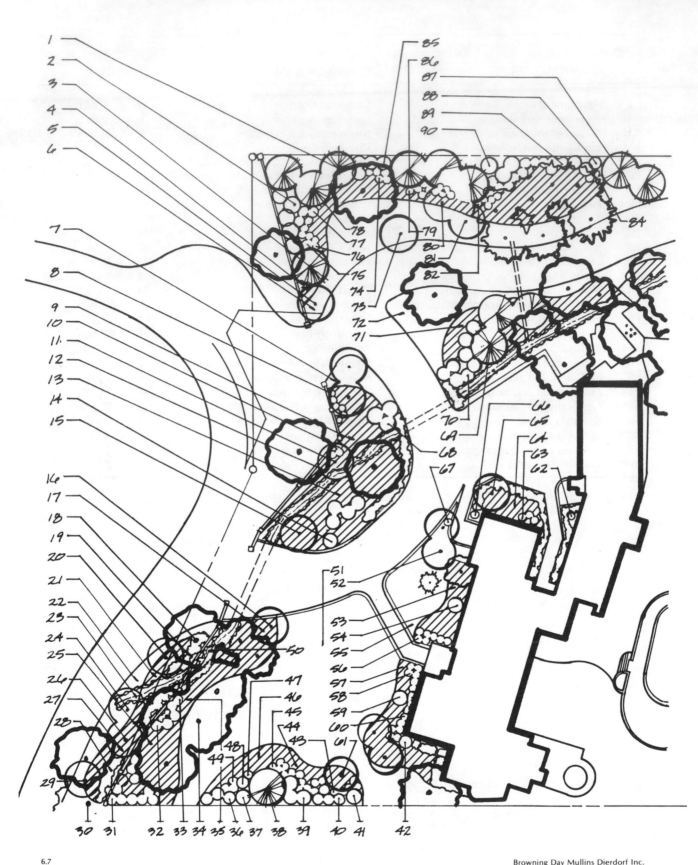

6.7

Browning Day Mullins Dierdorf Inc.

6.7 Because of the complexity of the planting for this residential estate, the landscape architect chose to use a series of numbers to identify each activity on the plan. These are explained in 6.8 (only part of the original is illustrated).

Landscape Plan Schedule

KEY QTY REMARKS

1 3   *Pinus strobus* (White Pine) 10'–12' ht. B&B or tree spade. Pines shall be inspected by the Landscape Architect before digging.

2 5   *Viburnum lantana* (Wayfaring Tree) 6'–7' ht. B&B Viburnums on site from Schnieder's Nursery.

3 1   *Pinus strobus* (White Pine) 10'–12' ht. B&B or tree spade. Pine shall be inspected by the Landscape Architect before digging.

4 3   *Taxus x media 'Sebian'* (Sebian Yew) 24"–30" sp. B&B.

5 3   *Cornus florida* (Flowering Dogwood) 8'–10' ht. B&B. Dogwood on site from Schnieder's Nursery.

6   Warren's A-34 sod (see sodding instructions).

7   Warren's A-34 sod (see sodding instructions).

8 7   *Taxus x media 'Sebian'* (Sebian Yew) 24"–30" sp. B&B.

9   *Cotoneaster horizontalis* (Rock Spray) 18" 24" sp. B&B or container; planted in staggered rows 24" o.c. (.29 plants per sq. ft.).

10   Prune dead from existing tree and raise limbs to 12' standard.

11   Existing Serviceberry (tagged "B") transplanted from in front of Simon house. (Oversize ball)

12 6   *Taxus x media 'Sebian'* (Sebian Yew) 24"–30" sp. B&B.

13   *Cotoneaster horizontalis* (Rock Spray) 18"–24" sp. B&B or container; planted in staggered rows 24" o.c. (.29 plants per sq. ft.).

14 5   *Viburnum plicatum 'Mariesii'* (Maries Doublefile Viburnum) 5'–6' ht. B&B. Viburnums to be inspected by Landscape Architect before digging. (Oversize balls)

15 1   *Corunus florida* (White Dogwood) 8'–10' ht. B&B. Dogwood on site from Schnieder's Nursery.

16 1   *Cornus florida* (White Flowering Dogwood) 8'–10' ht., B&B. (Spring only)

17   *Hedera helix 'Thorndale'* (Thorndale Ivy) 2¼" cells or heavily rooted cuttings approved by Landscape Architect planted in staggered rows 8" o.c. (2.6 plants per sq. ft.) (NOTE: groundcover instructions).

18   Prune dead from existing tree and raise limbs to 8' standard.

18   Prune dead from existing tree and raise limbs to 8' standard.

19   Existing, transplanted, and possible new yews forming yew grouping under the supervision of the Landscape Architect.

20 1   *Cornus florida* (White Dogwood) 4" cal B&B. Dogwood on site from Schnieder's Nursery.

21   (See Remarks for #17).

22   Warren's A-34 sod (See sodding instructions).

23   (See Remarks for #19).

24 1   *Cercis canadensis* (Eastern Redbud) 10' ht. clump; B&B Redbud on site from Schnieder's Nursery.

25   Prune dead from existing tree and raise limbs to 8' ht. standard.

26 1   *Cercis canadenis* (Eastern Redbud) 5" cal. B&B. Redbud on site from Schnieder's Nursery.

27   *Hedera helix 'Thorndale'* (Thorndale Ivy) 2¼" cells or heavily rooted cuttings approved by Landscape Architect planted in staggered rows 8" o.c. (2.6 plants per sq. ft.) (NOTE: groundcover instructions).

28   Existing, transplanted, and possible new yews forming yew grouping under the supervision of the Landscape Architect.

29 1   *Cercis canadensis* Eastern Redbud) 4" cal. B&B. Redbud on site from Schnieder's Nursery.

30   Prune dead from existing tree and raise limbs to 10' ht. standard.

31 11 *Philadelphus x virginalis 'Minnesota Snowflake'* (Minnesota Snowflake Mock-orange) 5'–6' ht. B&B.

32 4   *Philadelphus x virginalis 'Minnesota Snowflake'* (Minnesota Snowflake Mock-orange) 5'–6' ht. B&B.

33   (See Remarks for #19).

34   (See Remarks for #30).

35   (See Remarks for #17).

6.8

Landscape Plan Schedule, cont'd.

KEY QTY REMARKS

36 3 *Philadelphus x virginalis 'Minnesota Snowflake'* (Minnesota Snowflake Mock-orange) 5'–6' ht. B&B.

37 1 *Viburnum lantana* (Wayfaring Tree) 6'–7' ht. (B&B) Viburnum on site from Schnieder's Nursery.

38 *Pinus strobus* (White Pine) 12'–15' ht. B&B or tree spade. Pine to be inspected by Landscape Architect before digging.

39 3 *Viburnum lantana* (Wayfaring Tree) 5'–6' ht. B&B. Viburnum on site from Maschmeyer's Nursery.

40 4 *Philadelphus x virginalis 'Minnesota Snowflake'* (Minnesota Snowflake Mock-orange) 5'–6' ht. B&B.

41 1 *Viburnum lantana* (Wayfaring Tree) 6'–7' ht. B&B. Viburnum on site from Maschmeyer's Nursery.

42 1 *Viburnum carlesii* (Korean Spice Viburnum) 4'–5' ht. B&B.

43 5 *Spiraea nipponica* (Snowmound Spirea) 18"–24" ht. B&B.

44 Security camera.

45 12 *Spiraea niponica 'Snowmound'* (Snowmound Spirea) 18"–24" ht. B&B.

46 (See Remarks for #17).

47 1 *Spiraea nipponica 'Snowmound'* (Snowmound Spirea) 18"–24" ht. B&B.

48 1 *Philadelphus x virginalis 'Minnesota Snowflake'* (Minnesota Snowflake Mock-orange) 5'–6' ht. B&B.

49 3 *Spiraea nipponica 'Snowmound'* (Snowmound Spirea) 18"–24" ht. B&B.

50 (See Remarks for #19).

50 Warrens A-34 sod (See sodding instructions).

52 2 *Cornus florida* (White Dogwood) 8'–10' ht. B&B. Dogwood on site from Schnieder's Nursery.

53 (See Remarks for #17).

54 1 *Viburnum plicatum "Mariesii"* (Maries Doublefile Viburnum) 5'–6' ht. B&B. Viburnum to be inspected by Landscape Archtect before digging. (Oversize ball)

55 Warren's A-34 sod (See sodding instructions).

56 7 *Taxus x media 'Sebian'* (Sebian Yew) 18"–24" ht. B&B.

57 (See Remarks for #17).

58 6 *Taxus x media 'Sebian'* (Sebian Yew) 18"–24" ht. B&B.

59 (See Remarks for #54).

60 (See Remarks for #56).

61 3 *Cornus florida* (White Dogwood) 8'–10' ht. B&B. Dogwood are on site from Schnieder's Nursery.

62 1 *Pieris japonica* (Japanese Andromeda) 30"–36" ht. B&B or container.

63 3 *Pieris japonica* (Japanese Andromeda) 30"–36" ht. B&B or container.

64 (See Remarks for #17).

65 *Cercis canadensis* (Eastern Redbud) 2½"–3" cal. B&B. Redbud on site from Schnieder's Nursery.

66 (See Remarks for #62).

67 1 *Euonymus fortunei 'Vegetus'* (Biglead Wintercreeper) 18"–24" ht. B&B. Plant to climb on brick wall.

68 3 *Viburnum plicatum 'Mariesii'* (Maries Doublefile Viburnum) 5'–6' ht. B&B. Viburnums to be inspected by Landscape Architect before digging. (Oversize balls)

69 3 *Pinus strobus* (White Pine) 12'–15' ht. B&B or tree spade. Pines to be inspected by Landscape Architect before digging.

70 8 *Viburnum plicatum 'Mariesii'* (Maries Doublefile Viburnum) 4'–5' ht. B&B. Viburnums to be inspected by Landscape Architect before digging. (Oversize ball)

71 (See Remarks for #17).

72 Warren's A-34 sod. (See sodding instructions)

73 1 *Cornus florida* (White Dogwood) 5" cal. B&B. Dogwood on site from Schnieder's Nursery.

74 5 *Taxus x media 'Sebian'* (Sebian Yew) 18"–24" sp. B&B; 3' o.c.

75 1 *Lonicera tatarica 'Zabelii'* (Zabeli Honeysuckle) 4'–5' ht. B&B.

76 6 *Taxus x media 'Sebian'* (Sebian Yew) 18"–24" sp. B&B; o.c.

77 3 *Lonicera tatarica 'Zabelii'* (Zabeli Honeysuckle) 4'–5' ht. B&B.

78 (See Remarks for #17).

79	9	*Taxus x media* 'Sebian' (Sebian Yew) 18"–24" sp. B&B; 3' o.c.
80	1	*Cercis canadensis* (Eastern Redbud) 2½"–3" cal. B&B. Redbud is on site from Schnieder's Nursery.
81	1	*Cercis canadensis* (Eastern Redbud) 5" cal. B&B. Redbud is on site from Schnieder's Nursery.
82		(See Remarks for #74).
83		(See Remarks for #17).
84	4	*Taxus x media* 'Sebian' (Sebian Yew) 18"–24" sp. B&B; 3' o.c.
85	4	*Hamamelis vernalis* (Vernal Witch-hazel) 5'–6' ht. B&B. Witch-hazels are on site from Maschmeyer's Nursery.
86		(See Remarks for #1).
87		(See Remarks for #1).
88	3	*Hamamelis vernalis* (Vernal Witch-hazel) 5'–6' ht. B&B. Witch-hazels are on site from Maschmeyer's Nursery.
89	12	*Philadelphus x virginalis* 'Minnesota Snowflake' (Minnesota Snowflake Mock-orange) 5'–6' ht. B&B.
90	3	*Viburnum lantana* (Wayfaring Tree) 9'–10' ht. B&B. Viburnums are on site from Schnieder's Nursery.

12 TW
50 SCILLA EXCELSIOR
30 SCILLA ALBA MAXIMA
6 PF
5 RS
800 ENG. IVY TO FILL VOIDS
80 SCILLA ROSE BEAUTY
40 SCILLA ALBA MAXIMA
6 VG
5 TW
160 SCILLA EXCELSIOR
80 SCILLA ALBA MAXIMA
6 TW
5 PF
50 SCILLA EXCELSIOR
30 SCILLA ALBA MAXIMA
6 VC
50 SCILLA EXCELSIOR
30 SCILLA ALBA MAXIMA
70 SCILLA ROSE BEAUTY
30 SCILLA ALBA MAXIMA
2 PF
3 RS
5 VC
30 SCILLA EXCELSIOR
20 SCILLA ALBA MAXIMA
11 TW

PLANTER D   NORTH
SCALE : 1"=1'-0"

6.10

Browning Day Mullins Dierdorf Inc.

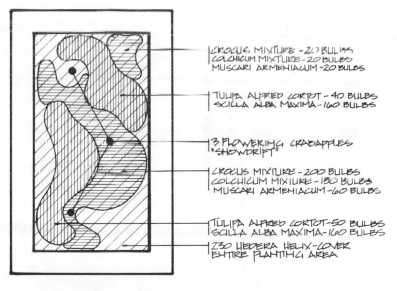

CROCUS MIXTURE - 200 BULBS
COLCHICUM MIXTURE - 20 BULBS
MUSCARI ARMENIACUM - 20 BULBS

TULIPA ALFRED CORTOT - 40 BULBS
SCILLA ALBA MAXIMA - 160 BULBS

3 FLOWERING CRABAPPLES "SNOWDRIFT"

CROCUS MIXTURE - 200 BULBS
COLCHICUM MIXTURE - 120 BULBS
MUSCARI ARMENIACUM - 60 BULBS

TULIPA ALFRED CORTOT - 50 BULBS
SCILLA ALBA MAXIMA - 160 BULBS

230 HEDERA HELIX - COVER ENTIRE PLANTING AREA

PLANTERS A, C, E
SCALE : ½" = 1'-0"

6.9

Browning Day Mullins Dierdorf Inc.

6.9, 6.10 *Planting plans for several raised planters in a downtown Fort Wayne, Indiana, governmental office complex.*

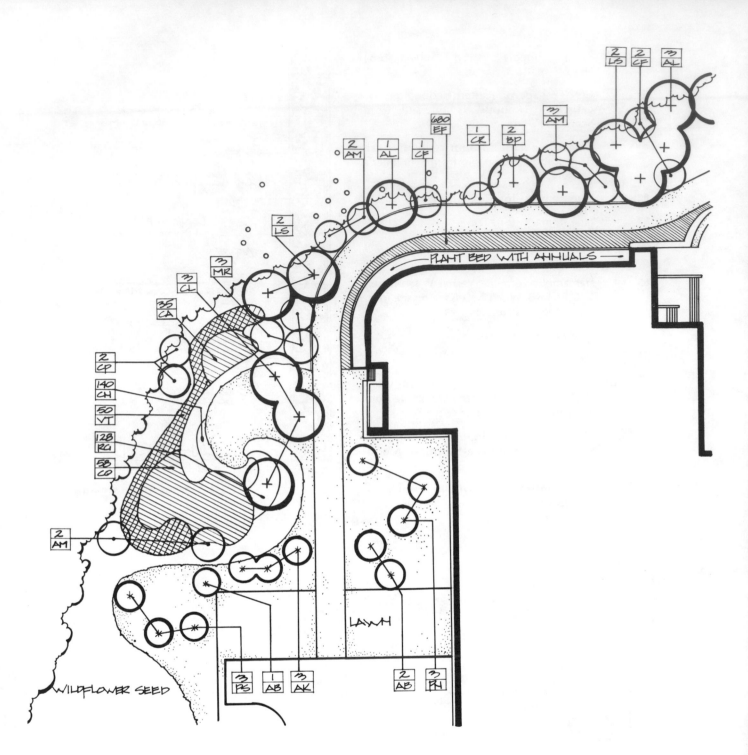

6.11

CR3, inc.

6.11 Planting plan for a large office complex for a life insurance company. The graphics were kept simple to make the plan easy to read.

6.12 Plant list for 6.11.

6.13 Plant list for the plan in 6.9.

Plant List

Key	Botanical Name	Common Name	Size
AB	Abies concolor	White Fir	8– 9′ ht.
AK	Abies koreana	Korean Fir	8– 9′ ht.
AL	Acer saccharum laciniata	Sweet Shadow Sugar Maple	4– 4½″ cal.
AM	Amelanchier canadensis	Shadblow	12–14′ ht.
BP	Betula papyrifera	Paper Birch	14–16′ ht. (clump)
CA	Clethra alnifolia	Summersweet Clethra	2½–3′
CF	Cornus florida	Flowering Dogwood	12–14′ ht.
CL	Cladrastis lutea	Yellowwood	3′– 3½″ cal.
CN	Centaurea dealbata	Persian Cornflower	Qt. pot
CO	Coreopsis verticillata	Tickseed	Qt. pot
CP	Crataegus phaenopyrum	Washington Hawthorn	12–14′ ht.
CR	Cornus florida 'rubra'	Pink Flowering Dogwood	12–14′ ht.
EF	Euonymus fortunei 'longwood'	Longwood Winter-Creeper	18–24″ spd.
LS	Liquidamar styraciflua	Sweetgum	4– 4½″ cal.
MR	Malus radiant	Radiant Crabapple	2½–3″ cal.
PN	Pinus nigra	Austrian Pine	10–12′ ht.
PS	Pinus strobus	Eastern White Pine	10–12′ ht.
RG	Rudbeckia 'goldsturm'	Coneflower	Qt. pot
VT	Viburnum trilobum	American Highbush-Cranberry	4– 5′

6.12

Plant List

WOODY PLANTS

No.	Key	Botanical Name	Common Name	Size	Remarks
25	PF	Pieris floribunda	Mountain andromeda	24″–30″	B & B
17	RS	Rhododendron schlippenbachii	Royal azalea	24″–30″	B & B
28	VC	Viburnum carlesi	Fragant snowball	24″–30″	B & B
80	TW	Taxus media 'Sebian'	'Sebian' Japanese yew	24″–30″	B & B
9	MS	Malus 'Snowdrift'	Snowdrift crabapple	2″– 2½″	B & B
2390		Hedera helix	English Ivy	2¼″ pot	9″ O.C.

FLOWERING BULBS*	Number	Remarks
Colchicum giganteum	380	Top size: plant
C. 'Waterlily'	130	6″ deep
Crocus 'Blizzard' (white)	100	Top size; plant
C. 'Early Perfection'	400	2″ deep
C. 'Golden Goblet'	160	
Muscari armeniacum	240	Top size: plant 2″ deep
Scilla 'Alba Maxima'	1700	Top size; plant
S. 'Excelsior'	910	4″ deep
S. 'Rose Beauty'	680	
Tulipa kaufmanniana 'Alfred Cortot'	270	Top size: plant 2″ deep

*Bulb note: All bulbs shall be spaced irregularly and be planted in drifts within shapes shown on plan. Crocus (15 percent white, 25 percent violet, 60 percent yellow) should be planted in many drifts, keeping colors separate. Scilla and colchicum varieties should also be separated into many drifts within the shapes shown.

6.13

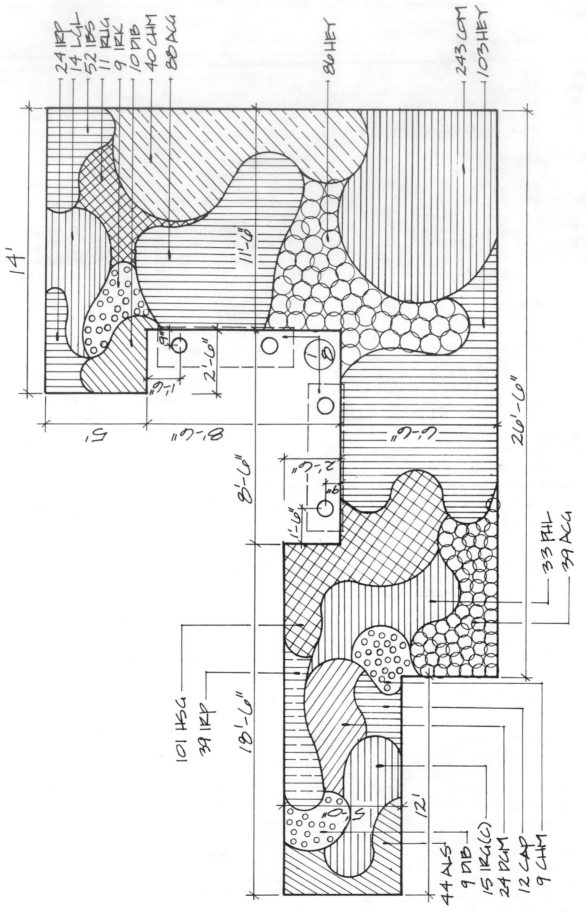

Browning Day Mullins Dierdorf Inc.

Plant list

Key	Name	Qty	Season	Color	Spacing	Height
ACG	*Achillea* 'Coronation Gold'	410	July-August	Yellow	8" O.C.	3'
ACT	*Achillea taygetea*	14	June-September	Yellow	8" O.C.	18"
ALS	*Alyssum saxatile (Aurinia saxatilis)*	467	May	Yellow	6" O.C.	1'
ASD	*Aster* (dwarf) 'Bonny Blue'	25	August-October	Lt. blue, lavender	12" O.C.	8"–10"
	A. 'Chorister'	25	August-Sept.	White	"	18"
	A. 'Pacific Amaranth'	25	August-Sept.	Purple, blue	"	15"
	A. 'Persian Rose'	23	Late Aug.-Oct.	Rose pink	"	12" – 15"
AST	*Aster* (tall) 'Blue Feather'	7	August-Sept.	Dark blue	"	22"
	A. 'Crimson Brocade'	10	"	Red	"	3'
	A. 'Lassie'	10	"	Pink	"	"
	A. 'Marie Ballard'	10	September-Oct.	Powder Blue	"	3'– 4'
	A. 'Patricia Ballard'	10	September-Oct.	Rose pink	"	24"–30"
	A. 'Peerless'	10	August-Sept.	Pale blue, lavender	"	24"–30"
CAC	*Campanula carpatica*	116	June-October	Clear blue	8"-10" O.C.	8"–10"
CAP	*Campanula persicifolia* 'Grandiflora Alba'	8	July-August	White	8"-10" O.C.	2'
	C.p. 'Grandiflora Caerulia'	18	July-August	Blue	"	57"
CHM	*Chrysanthemum maximum* 'Aglaya'	44	July-August	Double White	1' O.C.	–
	C. 'Thomas Killin'	128	July-Aug.	Sing. white/yellow	"	–
COM	*Convallaria majalis*	361	–	–	6" O.C.	–
DEB	*Delphinium belladonna* 'Clivedon Beauty'	67	June-September	Blue	12" O.C.	3'– 4'
DIB	*Dicentra eximea* 'Bountiful'	47	May-June (September)	Pink	10" O.C.	20"
DCM	*Doronicum caucasicum* 'Magnificum'	150	April-May	Yellow	8" O.C.	15"
HED	*Hemerocallis* (dwarf) 'Primrose Mascotte'	10	July	Yellow	18" O.C.	20"
HEY	*Hemerocallis* (pink) 'Artemis'	3	July-August	Orange-red	"	36"
	H. 'Magis Dawn'	6	June-August	Rose pink	"	"
HEY	*Hemerocallis* (yellow) 'Fascinating'	45	June (late)	Chinese yellow	18" O.C.	28"
	H. 'Hyperion'	45	July-August	Citron	"	40"
	H. 'Magnificence'	46	Early July	Burnt orange	–	"
	H. 'Perpetual Motion'	30	June-September	Apricot	–	–
HES	*Heuchera sanguinea*	360	June-September	Pink	6" O.C.	18"
HSG	*Hosta subcordata* 'Grandiflora'	228	August	White	"	"
IBS	*Iberis sempervirens*	367	May	White	"	12"
IRG (A)	*Iris germanica* 'Harbor Blue'	63	May-June	Sapphire blue	12" O.C.	2– 3'
IRG (B)	*I.g.* 'Judith Meredith'	27	"	Bright pink	"	"
IRG (C)	*I.g.* 'Olympic Torch'	15	"	Bronze	"	"
IRG (D)	*I.g.* 'Rainbow Gold'	12	"	Yellow	"	3'
IRG (E)	*I.g.* 'Solid Gold'	10	"	Deep gold	"	2'– 3'
IRK	*Iris kaempferi* 'Gold Bond'	20	June-July	White	10" O.C.	3'
IRP	*Iris pumila* 'Autumn Queen'	50	April-May	White	6" O.C.	Border
	I.p. 'Jean Siret'	95	"	Chrome yellow	"	"
6.15	*I.p.* 'Lieutenant Chavagnac'	50	"	Violet	"	"

6.14 Portion of a flower garden planting plan for a downtown urban park. This plan was designed for display of color through as much of the growing season as possible.

6.15 Plant list for the planting plan in **6.14**

Key	Name	Qty	Season	Color	Spacing	Height
IRS	*Iris sibirica* 'Royal Herald'	37	June	Purple	8" O.C.	36"
LGL	*Lavandula* 'Gray Lady'	48	July-August	Blue	12" O.C.	18" Border
LIE	*Lilium* 'Enchantment'	44	–	Red	6" O.C.	36"-40"
PAB	*Papaver orientale* 'Cavalier'	42	–	–	12" O.C.	18" Border
	P.o. 'Watermelon'	–		"	–	
PET (A)	*Petunia* 'Sugar Plum'	226	–	Pink-White	8" O.C.	–
PET (B)	*P.* 'Pink Cascade'	452	–	Pink	"	–
	P. 'Burgundy'	151	–	Burgundy	"	–
PHL	*Phlox paniculata* 'Balmoral'	185	July-September	Pink (dark center)	10" O.C.	3'
	P.p. 'Dodo Hanbury Forbes'	185	"	Pink	"	"
RUG	*Rudbeckia* 'Goldsturm'	75	August-Sept.	Gold	15" O.C.	"
	R. 'Robert Blum'	26	"	Pink	"	"
SAL	*Salvia* 'White Fire'	87	June-October	White	12" O.C.	14"
SOL	*Solidago* 'Peter Pan'	80	July-August	Yellow	8" O.C.	2½'
TEC	*Teucrium chamaedrys*	211	August	Blue	6" O.C.	12"

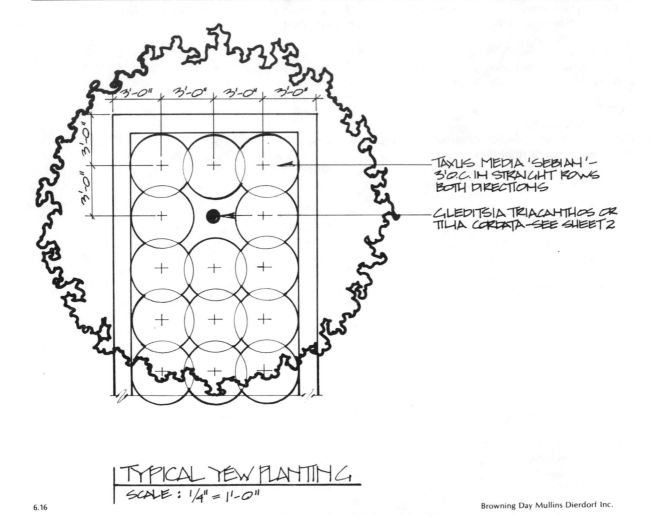

TAXUS MEDIA 'SEBIAN' – 3'O.C. IN STRAIGHT ROWS BOTH DIRECTIONS

GLEDITSIA TRIACANTHOS OR TILIA CORDATA – SEE SHEET 2

TYPICAL YEW PLANTING
SCALE : 1/4" = 1'-0"

6.16

Browning Day Mullins Dierdorf Inc.

6.16 *Planting plan for a raised planter in a downtown Fort Wayne, Indiana, governmental office complex.*

When the client can see the trees and shrubs in relationship to the rest of the features of the garden, such as in this perspective sketch, he/she will retain a better visualization of the potential finished project.

Janet Shen, Perkins & Will

123

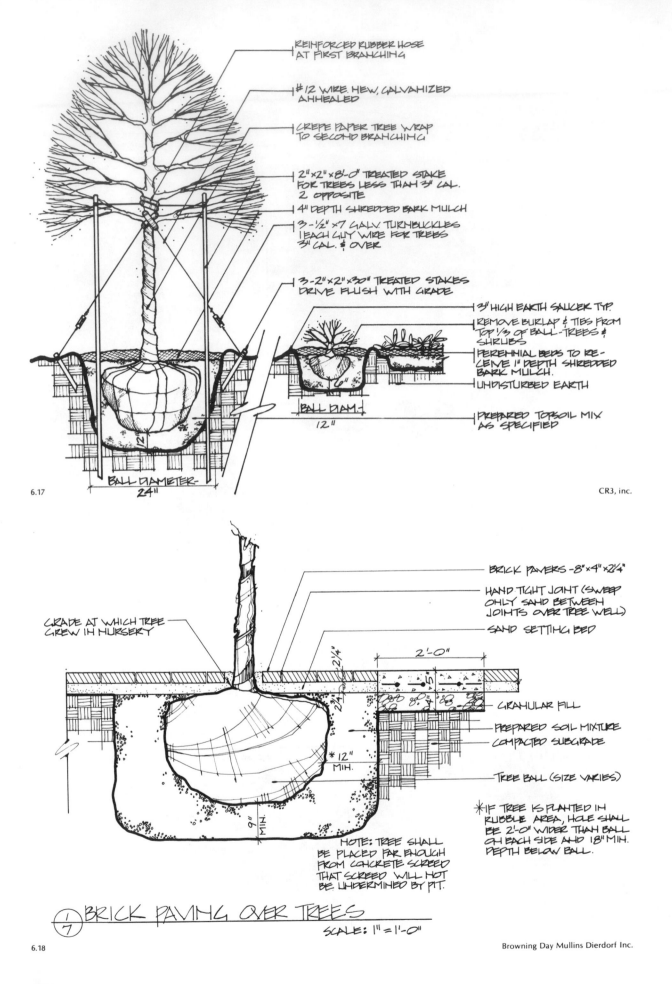

REINFORCED RUBBER HOSE
AT FIRST BRANCHING

#12 WIRE. HEW, GALVANIZED
ANNEALED

CREPE PAPER TREE WRAP
TO SECOND BRANCHING

2"x2"x8'-0" TREATED STAKE
FOR TREES LESS THAN 3" CAL.
2 OPPOSITE

4" DEPTH SHREDDED BARK MULCH

3-1/2"x7 GALV. TURNBUCKLES
1 EACH GUY WIRE FOR TREES
3" CAL. & OVER

3-2"x2"x30" TREATED STAKES
DRIVE FLUSH WITH GRADE

3" HIGH EARTH SAUCER TYP.

REMOVE BURLAP & TIES FROM
TOP 1/3 OF BALL-TREES &
SHRUBS

PERENNIAL BEDS TO RE-
CEIVE 1" DEPTH SHREDDED
BARK MULCH.

UNDISTURBED EARTH

PREPARED TOPSOIL MIX
AS SPECIFIED

BALL DIAM.
12"

BALL DIAMETER-
24"

6.17

CR3, inc.

BRICK PAVERS -8"x4"x2 1/4"

HAND TIGHT JOINT (SWEEP
ONLY SAND BETWEEN
JOINTS OVER TREE WELL)

SAND SETTING BED

GRADE AT WHICH TREE
GREW IN NURSERY

2'-0"

GRANULAR FILL

PREPARED SOIL MIXTURE

COMPACTED SUBGRADE

*12" MIN.

TREE BALL (SIZE VARIES)

*IF TREE IS PLANTED IN
RUBBLE AREA, HOLE SHALL
BE 2'-0" WIDER THAN BALL
ON EACH SIDE AND 18" MIN.
DEPTH BELOW BALL.

9" MIN.

NOTE: TREE SHALL
BE PLACED FAR ENOUGH
FROM CONCRETE SCREED
THAT SCREED WILL NOT
BE UNDERMINED BY PIT.

1/7 BRICK PAVING OVER TREES

SCALE: 1" = 1'-0"

6.18

Browning Day Mullins Dierdorf Inc.

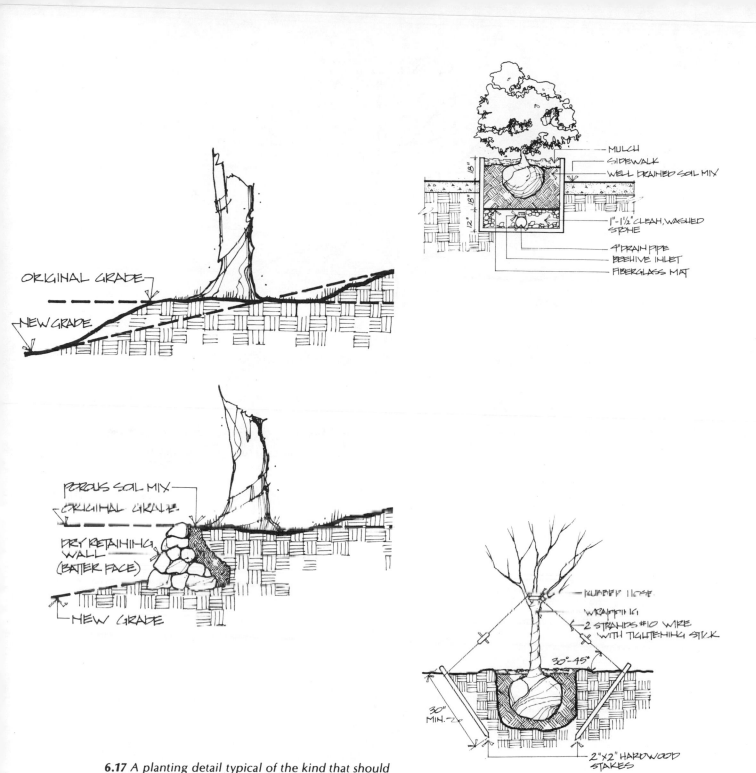

ORIGINAL GRADE

NEW GRADE

MULCH
SIDEWALK
WELL DRAINED SOIL MIX
1"–1½" CLEAN, WASHED STONE
4" DRAIN PIPE
BEEHIVE INLET
FIBERGLASS MAT

18"
18"
12"

POROUS SOIL MIX
ORIGINAL GRADE
DRY RETAINING WALL (BATTER FACE)
NEW GRADE

RUBBER HOSE
WRAPPING
2 STRANDS #10 WIRE WITH TIGHTENING STICK
30°–45°
30" MIN.
2"x2" HARDWOOD STAKES

3" BERM
BALL
SOIL MIX
120°

6.17 *A planting detail typical of the kind that should be shown on drawings among the contract documents. This specifies how a tree is to be staked, how earth saucers are to be created for each plant, the size of holes to be dug and the amount of mulch to be used.*

6.18 *Detail for installing a tree in a paving area.*

6.19 – 6.30 *A group of additional details which illustrate graphic techniques and variations for specifying tree staking, installing drainage pipe, plant spacing, use of backfill, etc.*

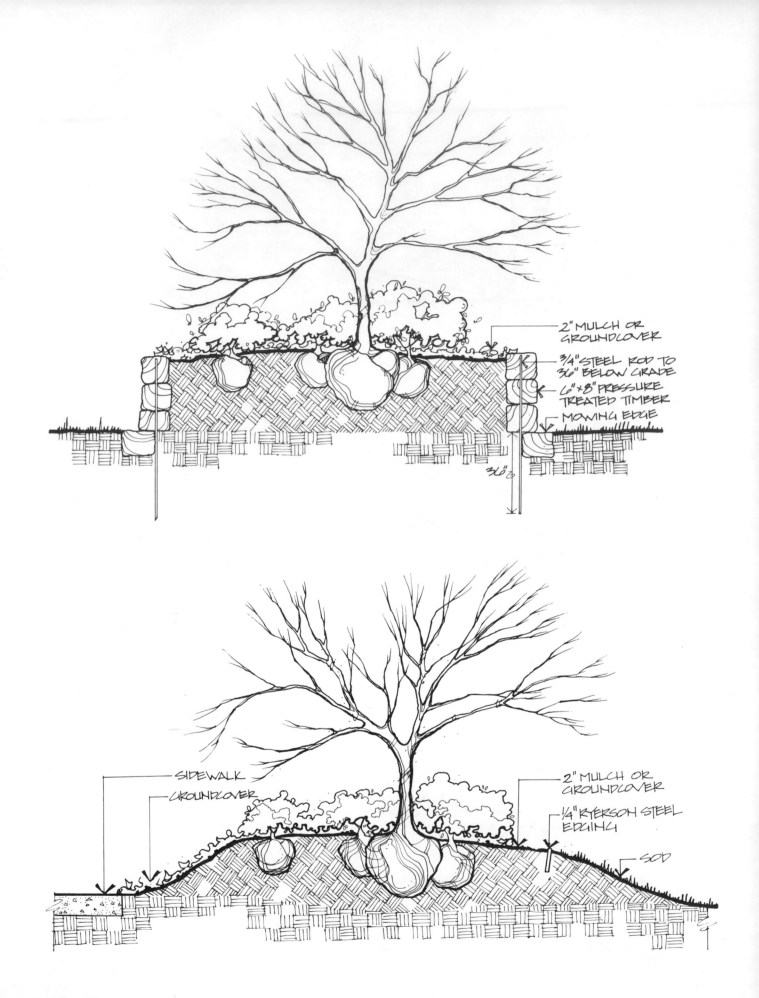

2" MULCH OR
GROUNDCOVER

3/4" STEEL ROD TO
36" BELOW GRADE

6"x8" PRESSURE
TREATED TIMBER

MOWING EDGE

36"

SIDEWALK

GROUNDCOVER

2" MULCH OR
GROUNDCOVER

1/4" RYERSON STEEL
EDGING

SOD

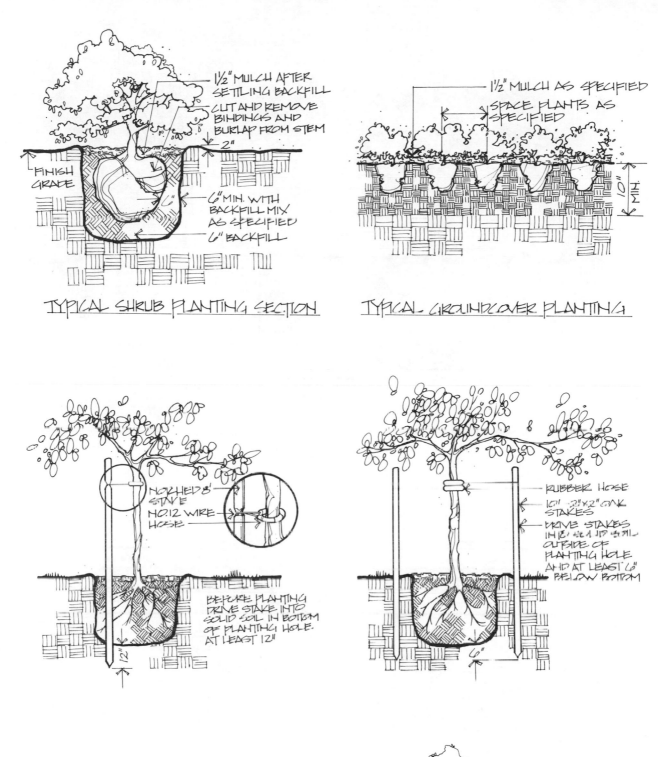

1½" MULCH AFTER
SETTLING BACKFILL

CUT AND REMOVE
BINDINGS AND
BURLAP FROM STEM

2"

FINISH
GRADE

6" MIN. WITH
BACKFILL MIX
AS SPECIFIED

6" BACKFILL

TYPICAL SHRUB PLANTING SECTION

1½" MULCH AS SPECIFIED

SPACE PLANTS AS
SPECIFIED

10" MIN.

TYPICAL GROUNDCOVER PLANTING

NOTCHED 8'
STAKE

NO. 12 WIRE
HOSE

BEFORE PLANTING
DRIVE STAKE INTO
SOLID SOIL IN BOTTOM
OF PLANTING HOLE.
AT LEAST 12"

12"

RUBBER HOSE

10' 2"x2" OAK
STAKES

DRIVE STAKES
IN 18' 4' 13' 5' 71"
OUTSIDE OF
PLANTING HOLE
AND AT LEAST 6"
BELOW BOTTOM

6"

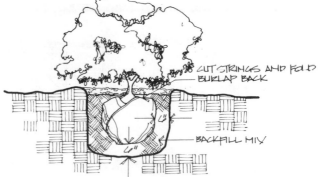

CUT STRINGS AND FOLD
BURLAP BACK

BACKFILL MIX

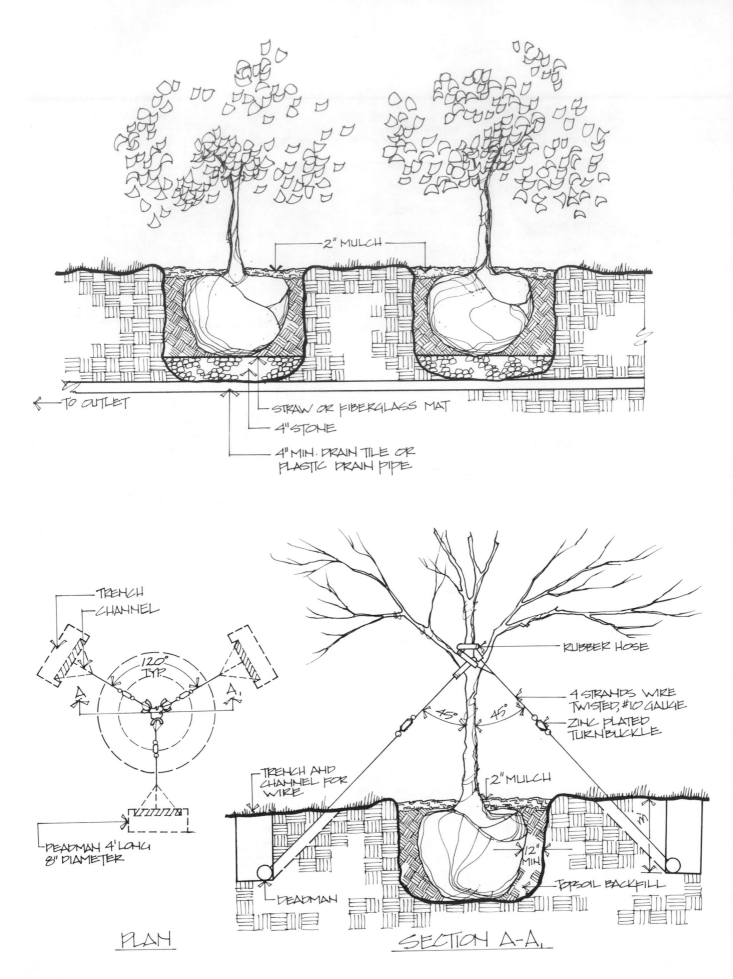

2" MULCH

TO OUTLET

STRAW OR FIBERGLASS MAT

4" STONE

4" MIN. DRAIN TILE OR
PLASTIC DRAIN PIPE

TRENCH
CHANNEL

120°
TYP.

A   A

DEADMAN 4' LONG
8" DIAMETER

RUBBER HOSE

4 STRANDS WIRE
TWISTED, #10 GAUGE

ZINC PLATED
TURNBUCKLE

45°   45°

TRENCH AND
CHANNEL FOR
WIRE

2" MULCH

12"
MIN.

DEADMAN

TOPSOIL BACKFILL

PLAN

SECTION A-A.

7

Preparing Specifications

SOURCES FOR GUIDANCE

Many helpful suggestions for writing specifications are available from the Construction Specifications Institute (hereafter we will refer to it as CSI), in Alexandria, Virginia. The institute publishes a *Manual of Practice*, as well as a number of other documents, and these are very useful as guidelines for the landscape architect. In "The CSI Format," a part of the manual containing model specifications, those for lawns and planting are listed at Section 0280 in Division 2, Site Work. Other specification lists that may be helpful are Section 0281, Soil Preparation; Section 0282, Lawns; Section 0283, Ground Cover and Other Plants; and Section 0284, Trees and Shrubs. Elsewhere in Division 2 are: 0210, Clearing of Site; 0220, Earthwork; 0250, Site Drainage; 0260, Roads and Walks; 0270, Site Improvements.

There are 15 other Divisions in "The CSI Format." Of these, Division 3 deals with specifications for concrete, and masonry is specified in Division 4.

In following the CSI suggestions, the planting specifications would consist of three parts: a general part, a discussion of products, and a discussion of execution.

WRITING SPECIFICATIONS

Specification writing is not easy. These have a style all their own; writing specifications requires utmost care because these serve as legal documents. Using the right words to say what is intended can have considerable effect on the quality of work performed, especially in any instructions that call for the contractor to exercise judgment. Even a misplaced comma can have drastic consequences, so careless use of punctuation and words should be guarded against.

A person without experience in planting design and construction cannot be expected to write specifications for this kind of work. The person who has that experience but who has not previously written specifications can use past specifications from other projects as a reference source. The experienced writer will assemble standard specifications from his experience and will build on these and modify them as needed for each individual project or set of circumstances.

Like all writing, the specifications begin as an outline from a collection of notes. From these, one or more rough drafts are prepared.

Much time can be saved by using a word processor. A master specification can be maintained on a floppy disk or other electronic data storage device and recalled for producing a modified yet original-to-a-specific-project set of specifications. The drugery of retyping is eliminated and a neat printout is obtained for reproduction of multiple copies for binding and distribution.

The final draft should be neatly and accurately typed. It may be typed on sheets which are photocopied or used for offset printing. Photocopying is good for small quantities; some processes and operators can produce very good quality copies. The best but most expensive process is offset printing. The quality is equal to the printed pages of a book. The finished specifications as they are printed are usually bound together in sets, once they have been duplicated, and are issued with the drawings to the bidders.

Too often landscape architects, because it is convenient or because of the pressures of time, use specifications prepared for previous projects without rewriting them. Each site will have its own unique problems, which must be dealt with, and accordingly it is advisable to write new specifications for each new project. A word processor makes it easy to prepare new specifications. The landscape architect who is striving to improve his work will find in helpful to solicit comments from each landscape contractor who constructs one of his projects. The comments may contain desirable suggestions about the specifications.

The appendices at the end of this chapter provide two widely different examples of specification writing. The first, from a private office, is simpler than the second. Because much private work is done with selected contractors, specification can be less specific or general. The second example is a set of standard specifications used by a state government agency. It is much more detailed and descriptive.

Appendix 7-A
Specifications – Private Office

Section 0280. Lawns and Planting

Part 1: General

1.01 Scope

a. Furnish labor, equipment, and materials necessary to complete the planting, maintaining, and guaranteeing of lawns and plants in accordance with the Drawings and as specified herein. The work to be completed in this section shall include the following:

1. Plants and Planting.

2. Lawns: seeding and/or sodding.

1.02 Agency Standards

a. **Nomenclature.** All plant materials used shall be true to name and size in comformity with the following standards:

1. *American Joint Committee on Horticultural Nomenclature.* 1942 Edition of *Standardized Plant Names.* (Published by Mount Pleasant Press, J. Horace McFarland Company, Harrisburg, Pa.)

2. *American Standard for Nursery Stock.* Copyright 1973. (Published by the American Association of Nurserymen, Inc., 230 Southern Building, Washington, D.C. 20005.)

Part 2: Products

2.01 Plant Materials

a. **Plant List:** A complete list of plants, including a schedule of quantities, sizes, and other requirements is shown on the Drawings. In the event that discrepancies occur between the quanities of plants indicated in the plant list and as indicated on the plan, the plant quantities on the plan shall govern.

b. **Substitutions:** No substitutions shall be accepted, except with the written permission of the Landscape Architect.

c. **Quality:** All plants shall be typical of their species or variety. All plants shall have normal, well developed branches and vigorous root systems. They shall be sound, healthy, vigorous, free from defects, disfiguring knots, abrasions of the bark, sunscald injuries, plant disease, insect eggs, borers, and all other forms of infections. All plants shall be nursery grown unless otherwise stated, and shall have been growing under the same climatic conditions as the location of this project for at least two (2) years prior to date of planting on this project. Contractor shall have the option of moving some selected trees from undisturbed portions of the site under the direction of the Landscape Architect in lieu of furnishing nursery grown materials. Plants which have been held in storage will be rejected if they show signs of growth during storage. Collected plants shall be taken from a subgrade favorable to good root development. All collected material shall be clean, sound stock and shall be free from decay.

d. Measurements: Size and grading standards shall conform to those of the American Association of Nurserymen unless otherwise specified. A plant shall be dimensioned as it stands in its natural position. Stock furnished shall be a fair average between the minimum and maximum sizes specified. Large plants which have been cut back to the specified sizes will not be accepted.

e. Preparation of Plants:

1. In preparing plants for moving, all precautions customary in good trade practice shall be taken. Workmanship that fails to meet the highest standards will not be accepted. All plants shall be dug to retain as many fibrous roots as possible. All plants shall be dug immediately before moving unless otherwise specified.

2. Balled and burlapped and balled and platformed plants shall have a solid ball of earth of minimum specified size held in place securely by burlap and a stout rope. Oversize or exceptionally heavy plants are acceptable if the size of the ball or spread of the roots is proportionately increased to the satisfaction of the Landscape Architect. Broken, loose, or manufactured balls will be rejected. Balled and platformed plants shall be securely tied with a stout rope to sturdy platforms equal in size to the diameter of the upperhalf of the ball of earth.

f. Delivery: All plants shall be packed, transported, and handled with utmost care to ensure adequate protection against injury. Each shipment shall be certified by State and Federal Authorities to be free from disease and infestation. Any inspection certificates required by law to this effect shall accompany each shipment invoice or order of stock, and, on arrival, the certificate shall be filed with the Landscape Architect.

g. Inspection: No plant material shall be planted by the contractor until it is inspected and approved by the Landscape Architect or his representative at the site of the project. The Landscape Architect or his representative shall be the sole judge of the quality and acceptability of the materials. All rejected material shall be immediately removed from the site and replaced with acceptable material at no additional cost.

h. Wrapping and Guying Details: Materials used in wrapping, guying protection, etc., shall be as specified herein.

i. Peat Moss: Peat moss shall be imported Canadian sphagnum peat moss, brown, low in content of woody material, and be free of mineral matter harmful to plant life. Peat moss shall have an acid reaction of about 4.5 pH, and have a water absorbing capacity of 1100 to 2000 percent by weight. Peat moss shall be thoroughly pulverized before use except when used as a top dressing. No native or sedge peats shall be approved. Top dressing shall be sphagnum chunks similar to "Professional Bale" as manufactured by Premier Peat Moss Co., New York, New York.

j. Herbicide: Use [locally recommended herbicide].

2.02 Lawn Seeding Material

a. Grass Seed: Grass seed shall be fresh, recleaned seed of the latest crop, mixed in the following proportions by weight, and meeting the following percentages of purity and germination. Seed shall be delivered to the site in the original unopened containers which shall bear the vendor's guarantee of analysis.

Grass Seed Mixture

Seed and Proportion	Minimum Purity	Germination
20% Park Bluegrass	90%	85%
20% Delta Bluegrass	90%	85%
20% Merion Bluegrass	90%	85%
40% Manhattan Rye	90%	90%

Substitute Creeping Red Fescue for Rye in areas of shade.

b. Mulch shall be clean straw or other materials approved by the Landscape Architect.

c. Fertilizer shall be 10-6-4 or approved alternate, and shall be delivered to site in unopened containers bearing manufacturers guaranteed analysis.

2.03 Sod Material (Alternate)

a. Sod shall be dense, well rooted sod, composed of 100% Bluegrass mix approximately two (2) inches high, grown in the general locality where it is to be used; it shall be free of debris, weeds, or other undesirable grasses. Submit mix to Landscape Architect for approval. The sod shall be cut out one (1) inch thick in uniform strips approximately 12" or 18" x 36", but no longer than is convenient for handling. Peat grown sod will not be acceptable.

b. Sod must be kept moist for protection and to facilitate handling. Sod shall be rolled in tight rolls or laid on boards or planks and lifted and transported to storage piles or carried to the point of installation without breaking or tearing. In all cases, sod must be lifted and loaded and unloaded by hand. Dumping from vehicles will not be permitted.

c. All sod shall be cut as required, and if possible shall be laid immediately. In no case shall sod remain in storage piles longer than three (3) days; sod shall be protected from wind and rain during such periods.

Part 3: Methods of Installation

3.01 Planting

a. **Time of Planting:** The Contractor shall start his planting when other divisions of this work, including placing of topsoil to finished grade, has progressed sufficiently to permit planting. Thereafter, planting operations shall be conducted under favorable weather conditions during the next season or seasons which are normal for such work as determined by accepted practice in the locality of the project. At the Contractor's option and full responsibility, planting operations may be conducted under unseasonable conditions without additional compensation.

b. **Layout:** Planting shall be located where it is shown on the plan except where obstructions overhead or below ground are encountered or where changes have been made in construction. Prior to the excavation of planting areas or plant pits, or placing tree stakes, the Contractor shall ascertain the location of all utility lines, electric cables, sprinkling system, and conduits so that proper precautions may be taken not to disturb or damage any subsurface improvements. Should obstructions be found, the Contractor shall promptly notify the Landscape Architect or his representative who will arrange to relocate the plant material. Necessary adjustments shall be approved by the Landscape Architect or his representative.

c. **Setting Plants:** No planting holes shall be dug until the proposed locations have been staked on the ground, by the Contractor, and until such locations have been approved by the Construction Superintendent or his representative. Each plant shall be planted in an individual hole as specified for trees, shrubs, and vines. All holes shall be dug with straight vertical sides and crowned bottoms, or as directed. All plants shall be set to ultimate finished grade, so that they will be left in the same relation to the surrounding grade as they have stood before being moved. No filling will be permitted around trunks or stems. All ropes, wires, staves, etc., shall be removed from sides and top of ball and removed from hole before filling in, unless otherwise directed by the Construction Superintendent. Burlap shall be properly cut and removed from sides of ball. When depth is specified, it shall be understood as meaning depth below finished grade. A layer of topsoil three inches thick shall be applied to the bottom of each hole and then lightly tamped. Excess excavation from all holes shall be removed from the site.

d. **Backfilling of Planting Pits and Planting Beds:** Use planting mixture of 4 parts topsoil, 1 part approved commercial horticultural peat moss. Existing subsoil to be removed from site by Contractor. Planting pits and beds shall be backfilled carefully to fill all voids and to avoid breaking or bruising roots. Tamp backfill firm to prevent settlement. When pit is nearly filled, water thoroughly and allow water to soak away. If settling of the backfill occurs after watering, add more backfill to bring to level.

e. **Trees:** All trees shall be planted in holes at least two feet greater in diameter than their ball of earth or spread of roots. The depth of the holes shall be at least two feet, and as much greater as is necessary to accommodate the roots, so that when the tree is placed therein it will not be necessary to raise or lower it to bring it to the proper finished grade. Topsoil shall be tamped under the edges of balled trees after inspection by the Construction Superintendent. Topsoil shall be backfilled in layers of not over nine inches in depth and each layer watered sufficiently to settle before the next layer is put in place. Enough topsoil shall be used to bring the surface to finished grade when settled. A slight "saucer," with a minimum of a 4" lip, shall be formed around each tree to hold additional water.

f. **Shrubs:** All shrubs shall be planted in holes at least one foot greater in diameter than the ball of earth or spread of roots. The depth of the holes shall be at least one foot and as much greater as is necessary to set the plant properly at finished grade. After preparation of the hole as specified, the plant shall be planted in the center of the hole. Roots of bare rooted plants shall not be matted together, but arranged in their natural position with soil worked in among them. The hole shall be filled with topsoil and settled thoroughly by watering. Area in shrub beds between shrubs must be spaded and pulverized to a depth of six (6) inches.

Arrangement of shrubs must meet with the approval of the Construction Superintendent. A slight "saucer" shall be formed around each plant to hold additional water. Shrubs shall not be planted closer than two (2) feet from the edge of shrub beds, nor closer than three (3) feet to walks or buildings.

g. Vines: All vines shall be planted in holes at least one foot in diameter and as much wider as is necessary to make them six inches wider than the size of pot or spread of roots. The depth of the hole and the manner of planting shall be the same as specified for shrubs.

h. Guying: All trees over seven feet (7') in height, and all pine trees, shall immediately after setting to proper grade, be guyed with three sets of two strands, No. 12 gauge malleable galvanized iron, in tripod fashion. Wires shall not come in direct contact with the tree, but shall be covered with rubber hose at points of contact. Wires shall be fastened in such a manner as to avoid pulling crotches apart. Stakes shall be of 2" x 2" lumber three feet long, or other material approved by the Construction Superintendent. Wire shall be fastened to stake at ground line. Stakes shall not be driven where utility lines are within five feet of finished grade, but shall be placed by digging holes for them. A board 1½ inches wide and 30 inches long of uniform thickness shall be hung on each wire. All guying shall be done to the satisfaction of the Construction Superintendent. All guy stakes shall be placed outside the perimeter of planting pits.

i. Wrapping: The trunks of all trees shall be wrapped spirally with two thicknesses of crinkled paper cemented together with bituminous material (or approved cloth serving same purpose) in strips 4 inches (4") wide immediately after planting, in a neat manner to the satisfaction of the Construction Superintendent to the height of the first branches, or as directed. Wrapping shall be securely tied with lightly tarred medium or coarse sisal yarn twine.

j. Mulching:

1. After planting has been approved by the Construction Superintendent a layer of commercial horticultural peat moss, two inches (2") thick shall be placed on the finished grade about all plants. The boundaries of this mulch shall be six inches greater in diameter than that of the hole. All shrub beds shall be completely covered with a similar material. [If permitted by law, some herbicides may] be incorporated into the mulch and used on all plantings that are tolerant of the herbicide as shown on the [herbicide] label. The amount of [herbicide] to add to a particular volume of peat moss is dependent on the area covered by that volume. The amount of [herbicide] to apply to one cubic yard of peat moss, assuming it covers 162 square feet at two (2) inch depth, is six (6) ounces. The peat moss should be removed from the bale and thoroughly loosened before mixing the [herbicide]. The volume of peat moss is measured while in the loosened stage.

2. The [herbicide] is thoroughly mixed into the peat moss just prior to applying to the planting. Before applying the mulch containing the [herbicide], thoroughly water the planting. If the [herbicide] label does not clear it for use on a particular species, use pure peat moss.

3. Top dress the peat moss mulch with sphagum chunks to a depth of 1½ inches.

k. Watering: Thoroughly water each plant immediately following planting.

l. Pruning and Repair: All plants shall be neatly pruned and/or clipped to preserve the natural character of the plants, and in a manner appropriate to the particular requirements of each plant, and to the satisfaction of the Landscape Architect. No plants shall be pruned or clipped prior to delivery except with the permission of the Landscape Architect. Broken or badly bruised branches shall be removed with a clean cut. All pruning shall be done with sharp tools in accordance with instructions of the Landscape Architect. Pruning cuts 2" in diameter or larger shall be painted over with approved tree paint. All accidental damage to trees and shrubs occurring during the course of planting operations, which is not so great as to necessitate removal of a branch or replacement of a plant, shall promptly be treated as required in accordance with recognized horticultural practices and the instructions of the Landscape Architect.

3.02 Seeding Procedure

a. Grass seed shall be sown in the Fall of [year] between August 20th and September 20th, or at other such times as approved by the Landscape Architect. Finish grading to the final 1½ inch shall be done by others.

b. Grass seed shall be sown evenly with mechanical spreader or by hand at the rate of four (4) pounds per one thousand (1000) square feet. All seeding shall be done on days when the wind does not exceed a velocity of five (5) miles per hour and the seed shall be dry or moderately dry.

c. Spread fertilizer at a rate of fifteen (15) pounds per one thousand (1000) square feet and incorporate into the topsoil uniformly.

d. After seeding, the surface of the soil shall be evenly raked with a fine-toothed rake or other procedures approved by the Landscape Architect.

e. Mulch shall be spread uniformly over all seeded areas at the rate of two (2) bales per one thousand (1,000) square feet.

f. Water mulch and seed bed thoroughly and immediately after completion of mulching. Soil shall be moistened to a depth of not less than four (4) inches. Contractor shall instruct Owner's representative on appropriate watering procedures during initial watering.

3.03 Sodding Procedures: (Alternate)

a. Sod shall not be laid unless soil is friable to a depth of six (6) inches.

b. A 25-5-10 fertilizer shall be incorporated into topsoil for new sodding at a rate of fifteen (15) pounds per one thousand (1000) square feet. At Contractor's option fertilizer may be spread after final rolling and before watering.

c. Finished grade shall be raked smooth, free from depressions or undulations, to the satisfaction of the Landscape Architect.

d. Rolling shall be done in two directions perpendicular to each other. The roller shall be a hand roller weighing not more than 200 pounds nor less than 150 pounds. After rolling repair and reroll any areas where depressions or other irregularities appear in the finished grade.

e. The soil surface shall be moistened immediately before sod-laying with a fine spray which will not cause disturbance of the finished surface.

f. Sod pieces shall be fitted tightly together so that no joint is visible and be firmly and evenly tamped by hand.

g. After sodding is completed and has been approved, it shall be rolled in the same manner as described in Paragraph **d.**

h. All sodded areas shall be watered immediately after final rolling with a fine spray to a depth of four (4) inches.

i. All sod shall be pegged on slopes steeper than 3:1.

Part 4: Maintenance, Inspection, Guarantees, and Replacements

4.01 Plants:

a. The Landscape Architect shall prepare a maintenance schedule for the Owner. The Contractor shall review and approve the maintenance schedule. The Owner will assume the responsibility of maintenance including watering, fertilizing, spraying, weeding, cultivating, repairing and tightening guy wires, etc., upon completion of planting. The Contractor shall periodically inspect the project during the guarantee period and immediately notify the Landscape Architect and Owner of any irregularities or deficiencies which will affect his guarantee.

b. The Contractor shall also be responsible for resetting of any plants to an upright position or to proper grade, and for the removal and replacement of any dead plant material.

c. **Guarantee:** All plants shall be guaranteed to remain alive and healthy for the full twelve (12) months period. Replacements shall be guaranteed an additional twelve (12) months.

d. **Inspection for Beginning the Guarantee Period:** Inspection of the planting work, to determine its completion for beginning the guarantee period, will be made by the Landscape Architect, upon notice requesting such inspection by the Contractor at least seven (7) days prior to the anticipated date. All planting must be alive and healthy in order to be considered complete. Each phase of this project will be inspected separately.

e. **Final Inspection and Replacements:** Inspection of the planting to determine its final acceptance will be made at the conclusion of the guarantee period by the Landscape Architect. No plants will be accepted unless they are alive and healthy. The Contractor shall replace any plants which are dead or, in the opinion of the Landscape Architect, are in an unhealthy or unsightly condition, and/or have lost their natural shape due to dead branches. The cost of such replacement(s) shall be borne by the Contractor and shall be included in his bid price for this section of the work.

4.02 Lawn:

a. Final inspection to determine final acceptance of the lawn shall be made upon written request by the Contractor to the Landscape Architect at least seven (7) days prior to the anticipated date.

Reprinted with the permission of Walker, Harris, Associates, Inc., Landscape Architects

SECTION 801 – LANDSCAPE EXCAVATION:

801-1 Description:

The work under this section shall consist of excavating areas to be landscaped in accordance with the details shown on the project plans and the requirements of these specifications. The work shall include the hauling and the satisfactory disposal of surplus excavated material.

801 3 Construction Requirements:

All landscape excavation shall be performed in reasonably close conformity to the lines, grades, dimensions and cross section established by the Engineer or shown on the project plans.

The hauling and disposal of surplus material shall be in accordance with the requirements of Subsection 103-3.03(E).

801-4 Method of Measurement:

Landscape excavation will be measured either by the cubic yard or by the ton.

Landscape excavation measured by the cubic yard will be measured in its original position by the Engineer, and the volume will be computed by the average end area method or by other methods approved by the Engineer.

Landscape excavation measured by the ton will be measured in accordance with the requirements of Subsection 109.01.

801-5 Basis of Payment:

The accepted quantities of landscape excavation, measured as provided above, will be paid for at the contract unit price per cubic yard or ton for the unit specified in the bidding schedule, complete.

SECTION 802 – LANDSCAPE GRADING:

802-1 Description:

The work under this section shall consist of grading, contouring, smoothing or otherwise shaping areas outside of planting beds and lawns at the locations designated on the project plans.

802-3 Construction Requirements:

Roadway shoulders and soil areas left exposed after planting shall be graded as required to leave a generally smooth appearance conforming to the general shape and cross section indicated on the project plans. The final surfaces shall be raked. All objectional material, trash, brush, weeds and stones larger than 2 inches in diameter shall be removed from the site and disposed of in an approved manner.

802-4 Method of Measurement:

Landscape grading will be measured either by the square yard of area actually graded or by the lump sum.

802-5 Basis of Payment:

The accepted quantities of landscape grading, measured as provided above, will be paid for at the contract lump sum price or the contract unit price per square yard for the unit specified in the bidding schedule, complete.

When landscape grading is not included as a contract item, full compensation for any landscape grading necessary to perform the construction operations specified on the project plans and the special provisions will be considered as included in the unit price paid for other roadside development contract items.

SECTION 803 – LANDSCAPE BORROW

803-1 Description:

The work under this section shall consist of furnishing, hauling and placing an imported material for plating embankment slopes, dikes and other designated areas in accordance with the details shown on the project plans and the requirements of these specifications.

803-2 Materials:

Landscape borrow material shall be secured from sources designated in the special provisions, from commercial sources or from contractor furnished sources. The material shall be in accordance with the requirements of Subsection 804-2.

803-3 Construction Requirements:

Prior to placing landscape borrow material the areas shall be cleared of all weeds, brush, trash, rock 2½ inches or larger in diameter and other objectional material.

The borrow material shall be spread and shaped to conform to the lines, grades and cross sections as shown on the project plans or as established by the Engineer. The material shall be watered and compacted in accordance with the requirements of the special provisions.

803-4 Method of Measurement:

Landscape borrow will be measured either by the cubic yard or by the ton.

Landscape borrow measured by the cubic yard will be measured in its original position by the Engineer, and the volume will be computed by the average end area method or by other methods approved by the Engineer.

Landscape borrow measured by the ton will be measured in accordance with the requirements of Subsection 109.01. The weight of the material will be determined by deducting the difference in weight between the average in-place moisture content of the material prior to pre-wetting and the average moisture content of the material at the time of weighing in accordance with the requirements of Subsection 206-3.

803-5 Basis of Payment:

The accepted quantities of landscape borrow, measured as provided above, will be paid for at the contract unit price per cubic yard or ton for the unit specified in the bidding schedule, complete in place.

SECTION 804 – TOPSOIL:

804-1 Description:

The work under this section shall consist of furnishing, hauling and placing topsoil in accordance with the details shown on the project plans and the requirements of these specifications.

804-2 Materials:

When a source of topsoil is not designated, the contractor shall furnish a source in accordance with the requirements of Section 1001. Topsoil from sources furnished by the contract shall conform to the following requirements:

The contractor shall furnish a written soil analysis prepared by an accredited soil analyst for each source of topsoil proposed for use. The soil analysis shall indicate the pH, total soluble salts, plasticity index and size gradation.

Topsoil shall be fertile, friable soil obtained from well drained arable land which has or is producing healthy crops, grasses or other vegetation. It shall be free draining, nontoxic and capable of sustaining healthy plant growth.

Topsoil shall be reasonably free from calcium carbonate, subsoil, refuse, roots, heavy clay, clods, noxious weed seeds, phytotoxic materials, coarse sand, large rocks, sticks, brush, litter and other deleterious substances.

Topsoil shall have a pH not lower than six nor greater than eight and the soluble salts in the material shall not exceed 1500 parts per million when tested in accordance with the requirements of [local test method].

The plasticity index of the topsoil shall be between 5 and 20 when tested in accordance with the requirements of AASHTO T 90 and the gradation shall be as follows:

Sieve Size	Percent Passing
2 inch	100
½ inch	85-100
No. 40	35-100

Certificates of Analysis conforming to the requirements of Subsection 106.05 shall be submitted to the Engineer for each source of topsoil proposed for use. The Engineer shall give final approval to each delivery of topsoil prior to use on the project.

804-3 Construction Requirements:

Topsoil shall be spread uniformly on the designated areas to the required depths. When necessary, the area shall be cultivated to a sufficient depth to break up any materials which may have been compacted as a result of the spreading operations.

The finished surface shall be free of all rocks larger than one inch in diameter.

804-4 Method of Measurement:

Topsoil will be measured either by the cubic yard or by the ton.

Topsoil measured by the cubic yard will be measured in its original position, and the volume will be computed by the average end area method or by other methods approved by the Engineer.

Topsoil measured by the ton will be measured in accordance with the requirements of Subsection 109.01. The weight of the material will be determined by deducting the difference in weight between the average in-place moisture content of the material prior to pre-wetting and the average moisture content of the material at the time of weighing in accordance with the requirements of Subsection 206-3.

804-5 Basis of Payment:

The accepted quantities of topsoil, measured as provided above, will be paid for at the contract unit price per cubic yard or ton for the unit specified in the bidding schedule, complete in place.

SECTION 805 – SEEDING:

805-1 Description:

The work under this section shall consist of furnishing all materials, preparing the soil and applying the seed to all areas designated on the project plans or established by the Engineer. Seeding shall be Class I, Class II or Class III, and shall be performed in accordance with the requirements of these specifications.

805-2 Materials:

.01 General:

Certificates of compliance conforming to the requirements of Subsection 106.05 shall be submitted.

.02 Seed:

The species, strain or origin of seed shall be as designated in the special provisions.

The seed shall be delivered to the project site in standard, sealed, undamaged containers. Each container shall be labeled in accordance with [your state statutes] and the U.S. Department of Agriculture rules and regulations under the Federal Seed Act. Labels shall indicated the variety or strain of seed, the percentage of germination, purity and weed content, and the date of analysis which shall not be more than 9 months prior to the delivery date.

Legume seed shall be inoculated with appropriate bacteria cultures approved by the Engineer, in accordance with the culture manufacturer's instructions.

.03 Mulch:

(A) General:

The type and application rate of mulch shall be as specified in the special provisions.

(B) Manure:

Manure shall be steer manure that has been well composted and unleached, and shall have been collected from cattle feeder operations. Manure shall be free from sticks, stones, earth, weed seed, substances injurious or toxic to plant growth and visible amounts of undercomposed straw or bedding material. Manure shall not contain lumps or any foreign substance that will not pass a ½-inch screen and when specified for lawn use, the material shall be ground or screened so as to pass a ¼-inch screen.

(C) Peat Humus:

Peat humus shall be natural domestic peat of peat humas from fresh water saturated areas, consisting of sedge, sphagnum or reed peat and shall be of such physical condition that it will pass through a ½-inch screen. The humus shall be free from sticks, stones, roots and other objectional materials.

Peat humus shall have a pH from 4 to 7.5 and the minimum organic content shall be 85 percent on a dry weight basis. The ash content as determined by igniting a five gram sample for, 20 hours at a temperature of 900 degrees F., shall not exceed 25 percent by weight.

Peat humus shall be furnished in undamaged commercial bales in an air-dry condition.

(D) Wood Cellulose Fibers:

Natural wood cellulose fiber shall have the property of dispersing readily in water and shall have no toxic effect when combined with seed or other materials. A colored dye which is noninjurious to plant growth shall be used when specified in the special provisions. Wood cellulose fiber shall be delivered in undamaged containers labeled and bearing the name of the manufacturer and showing the air-dry weight content.

(E) Straw:

Straw shall be from oats, wheat, rye or other grain crops of current season as approved by the Engineer and shall be free from noxious weeds, mold or other objectional material. Straw mulch shall be in an air-dry condition and suitable for placing with mulch blower equipment.

.04 Water:

Water shall be free of oil, acid, salts or other substances harmful to plants. The source shall be approved by the Engineer prior to use.

.05 Tacking Agent:

Tacking agent shall be as specified in the special provisions.

.06 Chemical Fertilizer:

Chemical fertilizer shall be a standard commercial fertilizer containing the minimum analysis and in the physical form as specified in the special provisions. Chemical fertilizer shall be furnished in standard containers with the name, weight and guaranteed analysis of the contents clearly marked. When a mixed fertilizer is specified, such as 5-10-5, the first number shall represent the minimum percent of soluble nitrogen, the second number shall represent the minimum percent of available phosphoric acid and the third number shall represent the minimum percent of water soluble potash.

805-3 Construction Requirements:

.01 General:

Seeding shall be of the class and variety specified, and shall be applied at the rate specified in the special provisions.

The contractor shall notify the Engineer at least two days prior to commencing seeding operations.

The planting season for all seed except Bermuda will be specified in the special provisions.

Seeding may begin earlier and/or continue later than the dates specified in the special provisions when approved in writing by the Engineer.

Bermuda seed shall be planted only at times when the daytime atmospheric temperatures are consistently above 90 degrees F, and the nighttime atmospheric temperatures are consistently above 60 degrees F.

Seeding operations shall not be performed when wind would prevent uniform application or would carry seeding materials into areas not to be seeded.

Preparation of the areas for the various classes of seeding shall be as specified herein and in the special provisions.

Equipment and methods of distributing seeding materials shall be such as to provide an even and uniform application of the seed, mulch and/or other materials in accordance with the specified rates.

Unless specified otherwise in the special provisions, seeding operations shall not be performed on undisturbed soil outside the clearing and grubbing limits of the project or on steep rock cuts.

.02 Classes of Seeding:
(A) Seeding (Class I):

Seeding (Class I) shall consist of furnishing and planting lawn seed.

Immediately before seeding, the surface area shall be raked or otherwise loosed to obtain a smooth friable surface free of earth clods, humps and depressions. Loose stones having a dimension greater than one inch and debris brought to the surface during cultivation shall be removed and disposed of by the contractor in a manner approved by the Engineer.

Where indicated on the project plans or specified in the special provisions, topsoil shall be placed and allowed to settle for at least one week prior to seeding. The topsoil shall be thoroughly watered at least twice during the settlement period.

Seed shall be uniformly applied in two directions at right angles to each other with one-half the specified application rate applied in each direction.

Immediately after seeding, the area shall be uniformly covered with screen manure at the rate of one cubic yard per 1,000 square feet and then watered until the ground is wet to a minimum depth of two inches.

Hydroseeding (hydraulic seeding) shall be an acceptable alternate for planting and mulching Seeding (Class I), using 1500 pounds of wood cellulose fiber per acre.

All machines used for hydroseeding shall be an approved type capable of continuous agitation of the slurry mixture during the seeding operation. Pump pressure shall be such as to maintain a continuous nonfluctuating spray capable of reaching the extremities of the seeding area with the pump unit located on the roadbed. The sprayer shall be equipped to use the proper type of nozzles to obtain a uniform application on the various slopes and at the distance to covered.

The seed, fertilizer, mulch, tacking agent (when required) and water shall be combined in the proportions of the various materials as provided in the special provisions and allowed to mix a minimum of five minutes prior to starting the application of the slurry. Seed shall be applied within 30 minutes after mixing with water.

Hydroseeding deposited on adjacent trees and shrubs, roadways, in drain ditches, on structures and upon any areas where seeding is not specified or is placed in excessive depths on seeding areas shall be removed.

Seeding areas flooded or eroded as a result of irrigation shall be repaired, reseeded and refertilized by the contractor at his expense.

(B) Seeding (Class II):
Seeding (Class II) shall consist of furnishing and planting range grass seed, flower seed and/or shrub seed, and includes mulching.

Where equipment can operate, the area to be seeded shall be prepared by disking, harrowing or by other approved methods of loosening the surface soil to the depth specified in the special provisions. On slopes too steep for equipment to operate, the area shall be prepared by hand raking to the specified depth. On sloping areas, all disking, harrowing and raking shall be directional along the contours of the areas involved. Loose stones having a dimension greater than four inches brought to the surface during cultivation shall be removed and disposed of in a satisfactory manner prior to grading and seeding. All areas which are eroded shall be restored to the specified condition, grade and slope as directed prior to seeding.

On cut and fill slopes the operations shall be conducted in such a manner as to form minor ridges thereon to assist in retarding erosion and favor germination of the seed.

Due care shall be taken during the seeding operations to prevent damage to existing trees and shrubs in the seeding area in accordance with the requirements of Subsection 107.12. Seed shall be drilled, broadcast or otherwise planted in the manner and at the rate specified in the special provisions.

The type of mulch, and the manner and rate of application shall be as specified in the special provisions.

Mulch material is placed upon trees and shrubs, roadways, structures and upon any area where mulching is not specified or is placed in excessive depths on mulching areas shall be removed as directed. Mulch materials which are deposited in a matter condition shall be loosed and spread uniformly over the mulching area to the specified depth.

During seeding and mulching operations, care shall be exercised to prevent drift and displacement of materials. Any unevenness in materials shall be immediately corrected by the contractor.

If a tacknig agent is specified in order to bind the mulch in place, the type, rate and manner of application shall be as specified in the special provisions. Prior to the applciation of a tacking agent, protecting coverings shall be placed on all structures and objects where stains would be objectionable. All necessary means shall also be taken to protect the traveling public and vehicles from damage due to drifting spray.

Unless otherwise specified in the special provisions, Class II seeding areas shall not be watered after planting.

(C) Seeding (Class III):
Seeding (Class III) shall consist of furnishing and planting range grass seed, flower seed and/or shrub seed, all without mulching.

Seeding (Class III) shall conform to the requirements specified under Subsection 805.3.02(B), except that mulching will not be required.

Unless specified in the special provisions, Class III seeded areas shall not be watered after planting.

.03 Preservation of Seeded Areas:
The contractor shall protect seeded areas from damage by traffic or construction equipment. Surfaces gullied or otherwise damaged following seeding shall be repaired by regrading, reseeding and remulching as directed by the Engineer.

805-4 Method of Measurement:

Seeding (Class I) will be measured either by the square foot of ground surface to the nearest 1,000 square feet seeded or by the lump sum.

Seeding (Class II) and Seeding (Class III) will be measured either by the acres of ground surface seeding or by the lump sum.

805-5 Basis of Payment:

The accepted quantities of seeding, measured as provided above, will be paid for at the contract price for the pay unit specified in the bidding schedule, complete in place.

No direct measurement or payment will be made for preservation or repairs of seeded areas.

SECTION 806 – TREES, SHRUBS AND PLANTS:

806-1 Description:

The work under this section shall consist of furnishing all materials and planting trees, palms, shrubs, vines, cacti and other plants (nursery stock) and transplanting trees, palms, shrubs, vines, cacti and other plants (collected stock and/or local stock), all as designated on the project plans. The work shall also include the preparation of planting pits, trenches and beds, including excavating and backfilling; the storage and protection of all planted and unplanted stock and other materials; all mulching, fertilizing, watering, staking, guying, pruning and wrapping; the cleanup of the area and disposal of unwanted and deleterious materials, all in accordance with the details shown on the plans and the requirements of these specifications.

806-2 Materials:

.01 General:

Certificates of Compliance conforming to the requirements of Subsection 106.05 shall be submitted to the Engineer for all contractor furnished materials, unless otherwise specified.

.02 Nursery Stock:

All plants shall be grown in a nursery and shall conform to the applicable requirements as specified in the current edition of "American Standard for Nursery Stock" as approved by the American National Standards Institute, Inc., and sponsored by the American Association of Nurserymen, Inc., subject to certain variations in size and measurement when specified on the project plans or in the special provision.

Botanical plant names shall be in accordance with the current edition of "Standardized Plant Names" prepared by the American Joint Committee on Horticultural Nomenclature.

All plants shall be true to type and species shown on the project plans and at least one plant in each group of plants of the same species delivered to the project shall be tagged with a weatherproof label stating both the botanical and common name of the plants in that group.

All plants shall be in healthy condition with normal symmetrical form, well-developed foliage, branches and cane systems at the time of delivery to the project. Plants shall be free from disease, insect eggs or infestations, disfiguring knots, bark abrasions, broken tops, branches or canes, damaged roots, sun, wind or frost injury; or other objectionable features.

Plants pruned from larger sizes to meet specified sizes will not be accepted.

Plants which are furnished in containers shall have been growing in the containers for a sufficient period of time for uniform root development throughout the plant's ball, but the roots shall show no evidence of having been restricted or deformed.

The presence of grass or weeds in the soil surrounding the plants may be cause for rejection of the plants.

No substitution of species and/or sizes of specified plants shall be made unless evidence is submitted in writing to the Engineer that plants in the species, quantity and/or sizes specified are not available during the contract period. The substitution of species and/or sizes shall be made only with the written approval of the Engineer prior to making said substitution.

All plants shall comply with Federal and State laws requiring inspection for diseases and infestations.

All shipments or deliveries of plant material grown within the State will be inspected at the nursery or growing site by the authorized State of [your state] authorities prior to delivery to the project. A copy of the state inspection record shall accompany all plant material grown out of state showing the plant material has been inspected for plant diseases and insects.

All rejected plants shall be removed from the project immediately upon rejection by the Engineer.

.03 Collected Stock:

Collected stock shall be secured from sources outside the project limits for transplanting, and shall comply with the size, type and species requirements designated on the project plans or in the special provisions. When sources for collected stock are not designated, the contractor shall furnish the source.

Collected stock shall be healthy, free from weeds, grasses insects, disease, defects and disfigurements, and shall be approved by the Engineer in their original position before transplanting operations are begun.

The contractor shall comply with all State and Federal laws regarding the removal, sale and transporting of native plants.

.04 Local Stock:

Local stock shall be secured from within the project limits for transplanting and will be designated on the project plans, the special provisions or by the Engineer. All plants shall be approved by the Engineer in their original position before transplanting operations are begun.

.05 Topsoil:

Topsoil shall conform to the requirements of Subsection 804-2.

Soil excavated from existing planting pits, trenches and beds meeting the requirements of Subsection 804-2 may also be considered and used as topsoil.

.06 Prepared Soil:

Prepared soil shall consist of a uniform mixture of topsoil, peat humus, manure chemical fertilizer, soil conditioners and/or other needed additives conforming to the specifications contained herein for the respective items and proportioned as specified in the special provisions.

Prepared soil shall be produced by combining the component materials into a homogeneous mixture. Prepared soil shall be mixed prior to placement in planting pits, trenches and beds. The Engineer shall be notified prior to the production of the prepared soil.

.07 Mulch:

Mulch shall conform to the requirements of Subsection 805-2.03

.08 Water:

Water shall conform to the requirements of Subsection 805-2.04.

.09 Chemical Fertilizer:

Chemical fertilizer shall conform to the requirements of Subsection 805-2.06.

.10 Lumber and Tree Stakes:

Lumber for header boards and stakes, and planter boxes shall be construction grade heart redwood, graded in accordance with the current Standard Specifications for Grades of California Redwood of the Redwood Inspection Service.

Lumber stored at the project site shall be neatly stacked on skids a minimum of 12 inches above the ground and shall be protected from the elements to prevent damage of warping.

Tree-stakes shall be sound, straight construction grade treated Douglas fir, lodge pole pine or of other species approved by the Engineer. Douglas fir stakes shall have nominal dimensions of 2 inches by 2 inches and lodge pole pine stakes shall have a diameter of 2 inches or greater. Tree-stakes may be furnished either rough or dressed. Type 1 stakes shall be a minimum of eight feet in length. Type 2 shall be a minimum of six feet in length and Type 3 shall be a minimum of four feet in length.

.11 Hardware:

Nails, lag screws, staples and other hardware shall be of galvanized commercial quality. All bolts and lag screws shall be furnished with galvanized malleable washers.

Wires shall be new 12 guage soft annealed galvanized steel wire.

Covers for guying wires shall be new, ½ inch minimum diameter vinyl or two-ply fabric bearing rubber hose.

806.3 Construction Requirements:

.01 Planting Season:

All planting shall be done during the time specified in the special provisions.

.02 Excavation:

The contractor shall be responsible for laying out all planting areas and staking all plant locations in reasonably close conformity to the dimensions and locations shown on the project plans. The Engineer will approve all planting areas and locations prior to any excavating of planting pits, trenches or beds.

In the event that field conditions exist that necessitate relocation of planting areas or locations, such as subsurface utilities, pipes, structures, impervious materials or inadequate drainage, the Engineer will designate new locations.

Prior to excavating planting pits, trenches or beds for plants, these areas shall be graded to the lines and grades designated on the project plans, or as established by the Engineer.

Planting pits and trenches shall be excavated to the dimensions indicated on the project plans or in the special provisions and shall have vertical and horizontal bottoms. When dimensions are not specified, the pits and trenches shall be excavated to a depth 12 inches below the root system and to a width twice the root system diameter.

When excavated material does not meet the requirements for topsoil as specified in Subsection 804-2, it shall be disposed of in a manner approved by the Engineer.

Excavation of planting pits, trenches and beds shall not be done when, in the opinion of the Engineer, the moisture content of the soil is excessive with respect to accepted horticultural practice.

.03 Shipping and Handling Plants:

Prior to shipping, all plants shall be dug, handled, prepared and packed for shipment with care and skill, in accordance with recognized standard practice for the kind of plant involved. The root systems of all plants shall not be permitted to dry out at any time. Plants shall be protected at all times against freezing temperatures, the sun and the wind while in transit. During transportation in closed vehicles, plants shall receive adequate ventilation to prevent "sweating." Plants delivered in a wilted condition will be rejected.

The contractor shall notify the Engineer at least 24 hours prior to the date of arrival of plants at the site. The Engineer will inspect all plants for conformity with the Specifications, and upon his acceptance, planting may begin. The Engineer may select at random no more than three container-grown plants of each species in every delivery to the site for root development inspection. If upon inspection of root development of plants so selected the Engineer determines the roots have become restricted or deformed in their containers, all plants of that species in that shipment, including the inspected plants, will be rejected and shall be removed from the site.

Deciduous plants may be furnished bare-root, and evergreen plants and conifers shall be furnished balled and burlapped or in containers, as specified in the special provisions or on the project plans. The balling and burlapping of trees and shrubs shall conform to the recommended specifications set forth in the "American Standard for Nursery Stock." All plant balls shall be firm and intact. Plants whose stems are loose in the ball will be rejected. All balled or burlapped plants shall at all times be handled by the ball and not by the top, leaders or canes.

All bare-root plants delivered in bundles shall have the bundles broken and the plants placed separately prior to being temporarily "heeled-in." Care shall be taken so that all plants removed from bundles will have an indentifying label. Bare-root plants shall be stored with roots completely covered with damp sawdust, soil or other suitable moisture-retaining material.

Plants delivered, inspected and found acceptable for planting shall normally be planted within 24 hours after deliver to the project site. Plants which cannot be planted within 24 hours after delivery shall be stored as specified herein.

Balled and burlapped plants shall have the root ball protected by moist sawdust, earth or other acceptable material.

All temporarily stored plants shall be protected from extreme weather conditions and roots shall be kept moist.

.04 Planting:
Planting shall not be done in soil that is excessively moist or otherwise in a condition not satisfactory for planting in accordance with accepted horticultural practice.

When an irrigation system is required in a planting area, it shall be installed and checked for coverage prior to planting.

Plants in containers shall be planted and watered the same day the container is cut.

Plants shall be removed from containers in such a manner that the root ball is not broken. Plants with broken root balls or with root balls that fall apart while being planted will be rejected.

Plants shall be planted plumb and shall be centered in the planting pit or trench.

Backfill material shall be prepared soil conforming to the requirements of Subsection 806-2.06 and shall be carefully firmed around the roots or the ball of the plant so as to eliminate all air pockets. Backfill shall not be compacted around the roots or ball of the plants during or after planting operations.

Plants shall be set to such depth that, after backfilling and watering, the top of the root ball and the level of the backfill will be at the surrounding grade as shown on the project plans. Any plant that settles below the specified grade shall be reset or replaced. Any additional backfill material required shall be prepared soil.

Immediately after planting, all plants shall be thoroughly irrigated until the backfill soil around and below the roots or the root ball of each plant is saturated.

.05 Pruning and Staking:
All plants shall be pruned in accordance with accepted horticultural practices. Pruning shall consist of removing all dead and damaged twigs and branches in order to form each type of plant to the standard shape for its species. All pruning cuts ¾ of an inch and over in diameter shall be treated with an approved tree-wound dressing.

Trees shall be supported in the manner detailed on the project plans or as specified in the special provisions.

Tree-stakes shall be driven vertically at least six inches in firm, undisturbed ground at the bottom fo the planting pit or trench. Stakes shall be positioned so as to clear the root system without disturbing the integrity of the roots.

Guying shall be as detailed on the project plans or as directed by the Engineer.

Tree ties and guy wires shall be periodically inspected and adjusted as necessary to prevent "girdling" or injury to tree trunks or branches.

After backfilling and prior to irrigation, trees shall be secured to stakes with tree ties in the manner detailed on the project plans or as specified in the special provisions.

.06 Care and Protection fo Trees, Shrubs and Plants:
Prior to the beginning of work under Section 807 – Landscaping Establishment, the contractor shall be responsible for the care and protection of trees, shrubs and plants planted under this Section. Such care and protection shall include, but not be limited to, the watering of stock, removal of trash and debris, controlling weeds, repairing, adjusting or replacing stakes and guying, furnishing and applying sprays and dust to combat diseases and insects and taking such precautions as necessary to prevent damage from cold, frost, sunburn or other hazards, all in accordance with the requirements of Section 807.

The contractor shall remove and replace, at his expense, all dead plants and all plants that show signs of failure to grow or which are so injured or damaged as to render them unsuitable for the purpose intended, as determined by the Engineer. The contractor may, with the approval of the Engineer, delay replacement of plants killed by frost until such time that frost is not imminent.

806-4 Method of Measurement:

Planting Trees, Shrubs and Plants, and Transplanting Trees, Shrubs and Plants will be measured on a lump sum basis, except that when the bidding schedule sets for specific items under this section on a unit basis, measurement will be made by the unit for each item specified.

806-5 Basis of Payment:

The accepted quantities of trees, shrubs and plants, measured as provided above, will be paid for at the contract lump sum price or contract unit price for the unit specified in the bidding schedule, complete in place.

No measurement or direct payment will be made for plants selected for inspection and not planted or for the care and protection of trees, shrubs and plants prior to the beginning of the Landscaping Establishment period, the costs being considered as included in the prices paid for plants accepted and paid for under the various contract items.

SECTION 807 – LANDSCAPING ESTABLISHMENT:

807-1 Description:

The work under this section shall consist of the care of all planted stock in accordance with accepted horticultural practices; keeping all horticultural and related activity areas free of weeds, grasses and debris resulting from the contractor's operations; applying all irrigation water; and the testing, adjusting, repairing and operating the irrigation system as it was designed to function.

The water used during landscaping establishment shall be furnished by the contractor or by the local government whose jurisdiction the project is within, as specified in the special provision.

807-2 Materials:

Materials necessary for the establishment of the seeding and planted stock, and the operations of the irrigation system shall be furnished at no additional cost by the contractor and shall conform to the requirements of these specifications and the special provisions.

807-3 Construction Requirements:

.01 General:

The work period for landscaping establishment shall be the number of calendar days specified in the special provisions. The work period shall begin after all other work under the contract has been completed and only when the Engineer is assured that the work can be performed in a continuous and consistent manner without restricting the use of any facilities by the traveling public.

Each calendar day during which the Engineer determines that no work under landscaping establishment is required, and the contractor is so advised, regardless of whether or not the contractor performs landscaping establishment work, will be used to reduce the total number of calendar days specified.

Each calendar day during which the Engineer determines that work under landscaping establishment is required, and the contractor is so advised, and the contractor fails to accomplish the required work, will not be used to reduce the total number of calendar days specified.

Thirty calendar days after the beginning of the landscaping establishment period and at the end of every 30 calendar days the Engineer, accompanied by the contractor, will inspect all planted stock and the irrigation system. The Engineer will notify the contractor at least one week in advance of the date for each inspection. The final inspection will be made approximately 21 calendar days from the expected termination of the landscaping establishment period.

A special inspection will be required at anytime during the landscaping establishment period when, in the opinion of the Engineer, conditions justify such action.

The contractor will not be required to keep the planted areas cleared of trash and debris unless such trash and debris is a result of his operations. If, in the opinion of the Engineer, trash and debris has been deposited within the planted areas, not as a result of the contractor's operation, which trash and debris is detrimental to the health and proper development of the plant material, the Engineer may require the contractor to clear the areas of this material.

.02 Planted Stock and Seeding Establishment:

All dead or unhealthy stock shall be removed and replaced, as directed, at the contractor's expense, within 21 calendar days from the date of the inspection and the contractor shall notify the Engineer in writing when the replacement work has been performed. Stock furnished for replacement shall be of the same size and species as originally specified.

After the final inspection and all dead or unhealthy stock has been removed, and, if directed, replaced, the contractor will then no longer be responsible for the replacement of stock.

In the case of certain stock found to be dead or unhealthy at the inspections specified above, the contractor may be ordered to remove certain dead or unhealthy stock and may be ordered not to replace such stock when nonreplacement would not adversely affect the planting design. The initial furnishing and planting, and the subsequent removal of such stock ordered removed and not replaced shall be at the contractor's expense.

Unless otherwise specified, all areas within the outer boundary of tree and shrub basins, grass areas, decomposed granite areas, rock mulched areas and areas within the perimeter of mass plantings shall be kept cleared of weeds and other undesirable vegetation. The boundaries for tree and shrub basis shall be the circumference of circles with five-foot radii having as centers the trunk or main stem. The boundaries for other areas shall consist of lines passing through points three feet beyond the outside edges of the planted, decomposed granite or rock-mulched areas.

The control of weeds shall be accomplished either by the use of herbicides or by manual means. The types of herbicides to be used and the methods of application shall be in conformity with the Environmental Protection Agency requirements, labeling instructions, and shall be approved by the Engineer. The contractor shall keep a record of all applications; the type of herbicides used, such as pre- or post-emergent; the rate and method of applications; and the date and location of such applications. A copy of this record shall be submitted to the Engineer every month.

A final, thorough weeding to remove all weeds and undesirable grasses from planted areas shall be performed within ten days of the termination of the landscaping establishment period.

Lawn areas shall be mowed, weeded, edged and trimmed at the time in accordance with standard horticultural procedures. Watering and fertilizing of lawns shall be done at intervals as necessary to maintain a good color and sturdy growth.

The contractor shall water and maintain the seeded area to provide a uniform and satisfactory stand of grass. To be acceptable, lawns shall have a good, uniform color and sturdy growth. At least 98 percent of the area designated to be planted shall have an acceptable lawn.

.03 Irrigation System Establishment:

The irrigation system shall be tested, adjusted, repaired, and operated in the manner it was designed to function and as it was accepted under the contract items of work. Components such as backflow prevention units and pressure reducing valves as well as all other appurtenances shall function properly in accordance with the requirements of the design and the special provisions, together with the recommendations of the manufacturer. No change in the system as it was accepted under the contract shall be made without written approval of the Engineer.

The irrigation system shall be tested within one week prior to each scheduled inspection. Testing of the various components shall be as specified in the special provisions or as directed by the Engineer. The contractor shall keep a record of the results of all testing and shall submit a copy of these results to the Engineer upon completion of each test.

807-4 Method of Measurement:

Landscaping establishment will be measured as a single lump sum unit of work.

807-5 Basis of Payment:

The accepted landscaping establishment, measured as provided above, will be paid for at the contract lump sum price specified in the bidding schedule, complete.

Partial payments may be made for landscaping establishment. Payment will be based upon the length of the landscaping establishment period, as specified in the special provisions, and the contract lump sum price for the item.

If the contractor furnishes the water used during landscaping establishment, the cost shall be considered included in the lump sum price bid for this item.

Payment for removal of trash and debris deposited within the planted areas, not as a result of the contractor's operation, will be made in accordance with the requirements of Subsection 109.04.

SECTION 808 – LANDSCAPE IRRIGATION SYSTEM:

The specification for furnishing and installing a water distribution system and/or a landscape irrigation system will be provided as a special provision in the contract.

Acknowledgments

Quite a number of individuals influenced the development of this book. The list includes colleagues both in the practicing profession and academia, former instructors, clients with unique needs, and students whose probing questions stimulated new ideas and approaches.

A special thanks to those professional firms who provided examples of their work for reproduction herein. Their names appear in small print in the lower right corner of their work. Photographers are also credited in the lower right hand corner, and the author is grateful for permission to use their work. All photographs not credited are the work of the author, and appreciation is due to the many professionals whose unidentified projects are the subject of those photographs. They contribute much to the visual content of this book.

The sketches and drawings not otherwise credited are the work of Cathy Lambert.

TABLES OF MEASUREMENT

Weights

English (Avoirdupois)
1 ton	= 2,000 pounds
1 pound	= 16 ounces
1 ounce	= 16 drams
1 dram	= 27.34 grains

Metric
1 ton	= 1,000 Kilograms
1 kilogram	= 1,000 grams
1 gram	= 1,000 milligrams

Liquid

1 gallon	= 4 quarts
1 quart	= 2 pints
1 pint	= 16 fluid ounces

1 liter	= 1,000 milliliters

Length

1 mile	= 5,280 feet
1 furlong	= 40 rods
1 rod	= 5½ yards
1 yard	= 3 feet
1 foot	= 12 inches

1 kilometer	= 1,000 meters
1 meter	= 100 centimeters
1 centimeter	= 10 millimeters

Surface

1 square mile	= 640 acres
1 acre	= 43,560 square feet
1 square yard	= 9 square feet
1 square foot	= 144 square inches

1 square kilometer	= 100 hectares
1 hectare	= 10,000 square meters

MEASUREMENT EQUIVALENTS

Length

Meter	= 1.093 yards
	= 3.281 feet
	= 39.370 inches
Kilometer	= 0.621 mile

Yard	= 0.9144 meter
Foot	= 0.3048 meter
Inch	= 0.0254 meter
Mile	= 1.609 kilometers

MEASUREMENT EQUIVALENTS (Continued)

Metric (cont.)

English (cont.)

Surface

Square meter	= 1.196 square yards	Square yard	= 0.836 square meter
	= 10.764 square feet	Square foot	= 0.092 square meter
Square centimeter	= 0.155 square inch	Square inch	= 6.45 square centimeters
Square kilometer	= 0.386 square mile	Square mile	= 2.590 square kilometers
Hectare	= 2.471 acres	Acre	= 0.405 hectare

Volume

Cubic meter	= 1.308 cubic yards	Cubic yard	= 0.764 cubic meter
	= 35.314 cubic feet	Cubic foot	= 0.028 cubic meter
Cubic centimeter	= 0.061 cubic inch	Cubic inch	= 16.387 cubic centimeters
Stere	= 0.275 cord (wood)	Cord	= 3.624 steres

Capacity

Liter	= 1.056 U.S. liquid quarts	U.S. liquid quart	= 0.946 liter
	or 0.880 English liquid quart	Dry quart	= 1.111 liters
	= 0.908 dry quart	U.S. gallon	= 3.785 liters
	= 0.264 U.S. gallon or	English gallon	= 4.543 liters
	= 0.220 English gallon	U.S. bushel	= 0.352 hectoli
Hectoliter	= 2.837 U.S. bushels or	English bushel	= 0.363 hectoli
	= 2.75 English bushels		

Weight

Gram	= 15.432 grains	Grain	= 0.0648 gram
	= 0.032 troy ounce	Troy ounce	= 31.103 grams
	= 0.0352 avoirdupois ounce	Avoirdupois ounce	= 28.35 grams
Kilogram	= 2.2046 pounds avoirdupois	Pound	= 0.4536 kilogram
Metric ton	= 2204.62 pounds avoirdupois	Short ton	= 0.907 metric
Carat	= 3.08 grains avoirdupois		

CONVERSION FACTORS

When you know:	You can find:	If you multiply by:
Area		
acres	sq. feet	43,560.
acres	sq. meters	4,046.8
sq. centimeters	sq. feet	0.00108
sq. centimeters	sq. inches	0.1550
sq. feet	sq. centimeters	929.03
sq. feet	sq. inches	144.
sq. feet	sq. meters	0.0929
sq. feet	sq. yards	0.1111
sq. inches	sq. centimeters	6.4516
sq. inches	sq. feet	0.00694
sq. inches	sq. meters	0.000645
sq. meters	sq. feet	10.764
sq. meters	sq. yards	1.196
sq. yards	sq. feet	9.
sq. yards	sq. meters	0.8361
Length		
centimeters	inches	0.3937
centimeters	yards	0.01094
feet	inches	12.0
feet	meters	0.30481
feet	yards	0.333
inches	centimeters	2.540
inches	feet	0.08333
inches	meters	0.02540
inches	millimeters	25.400
inches	yards	0.2778
kilometers	feet	3,281.
kilometers	miles (nautical)	0.5336
kilometers	miles (statute)	0.6214
kilometers	yards	1,094.
meters	feet	3.2809
meters	yards	1.0936
miles (statute)	feet	5,280.
miles (statute)	kilometers	1.6093
miles (statute)	meters	1,609.34
miles (statute)	yards	1,760.
miles (nautical)	feet	6,080.2
miles (nautical)	kilometers	1.8520
miles (nautical)	meters	1,852.0
millimeters	inches	0.03937
rods	meters	5.0292
yards	centimeters	91.44
yards	feet	3.0
yards	inches	36.0
yards	meters	0.9144
Pressure		
grams per cu. cm.	oz. per cu. in.	0.5780
kilograms per sq. cm.	pounds per sq. in.	14.223
kilograms per sq. meter	pounds per sq. ft.	0.2048
kilograms per sq. meter	pounds per sq. yd.	1.8433
kilograms per cu. meter	pounds per cu. ft.	0.06243
ounces per cu. in.	grams per cu. cm.	1.7300
pounds per cu. ft.	kilograms per cu. meter	16.019
pounds per sq. ft.	kilograms per sq. meter	4.8824
pounds per sq. in.	kilograms per sq. cm.	0.0703
pounds per sq. yd.	kilograms per sq. meter	0.5425

CONVERSION FACTORS (Continued)

When you know:	You can find:	If you multiply by:
Velocity		
feet per minute	meters per sec.	0.00508
feet per second	meters per sec.	0.3048
inches per second	meters per sec.	0.0254
kilometers per hour	meters per sec.	0.2778
knots	meters per sec.	0.5144
miles per hour	meters per sec.	0.4470
miles per minute	meters per sec.	26.8224
Volume		
cubic centimeters	cubic inches	0.06102
cubic feet	cubic inches	1,728.0
cubic feet	cubic meters	0.0283
cubic feet	cubic yards	0.0370
cubic feet	gallons	7.481
cubic feet	liters	28.32
cubic feet	quarts	29.9222
cubic inches	cubic centimeters	16.39
cubic inches	cubic feet	0.0005787
cubic inches	cubic meters	0.00001639
cubic inches	liters	0.0164
cubic inches	gallons	0.004329
cubic inches	quarts	0.01732
cubic meters	cubic feet	35.31
cubic meters	cubic inches	61,023.
cubic meters	cubic yards	1.3087
cubic yards	cubic feet	27.0
cubic yards	cubic meters	0.7641
gallons	cubic feet	0.1337
gallons	cubic inches	231.0
gallons	cubic meters	0.003785
gallons	liters	3.785
gallons	quarts	4.0
liters	cubic feet	0.03531
liters	cubic inches	61.017
liters	gallons	0.2642
liters	pints	2.1133
liters	quarts	1.057
liters	cubic meters	0.0010
pints	cubic meters	0.004732
pints	liters	0.4732
pints	quarts	0.50
quarts	cubic feet	0.03342
quarts	cubic inches	57.75
quarts	cubic meters	0.0009464
quarts	gallons	0.25
quarts	liters	0.9464
quarts	pints	2.0
Weight		
grams	kilograms	0.001
grams	ounces	0.03527
grams	pounds	0.002205
kilograms	ounces	35.274
kilograms	pounds	2.2046
ounces	grams	28.35
ounces	kilograms	0.02835
ounces	pounds	0.0625
pounds	grams	453.6
pounds	kilograms	0.4536
pounds	ounces	16.0

Index